THE
PLANT LOVER'S GUIDE
TO
TULIPS

THE **PLANT LOVER'S GUIDE** TO
TULIPS

RICHARD WILFORD

TIMBER PRESS
PORTLAND · LONDON

CONTENTS

69
100 Tulips for the Garden

183
Growing and Propagating

WHY I LOVE TULIPS

How can you not love a perfect display of bright, pristine tulips, basking in the warmth of the spring sunshine?

The richness of their colours and the variety of their flower shapes make tulips endlessly fascinating. It may not be love at first sight, but the allure of these plants will creep up on you and before you know it, you are seeking out new varieties, experimenting with different colour combinations, and finding new places to try tulips in your garden.

I first started paying attention to tulips when I was looking after the bulb collections at the Royal Botanic Gardens, Kew. One of the cold frames was home to a collection of tulip species growing in clay pots. I watered them, repotted them every autumn, and put them out on display when they flowered, as I did with all the other bulbs. Not until I saw a tulip growing in the wild, however, did I really start to take more notice.

It was on the Mediterranean island of Crete that I saw my first wild tulip. It was tiny—a delicate, pale pink flower, almost white, held on a short stem above two narrow leaves. Its name was *Tulipa cretica* and it seemed to be growing straight out of a rock, surviving on the bare minimum of soil.

My first wild tulip, *Tulipa cretica*, growing out of a rock on the Mediterranean island of Crete

The pink-and-yellow blooms of *Tulipa saxatilis*

The Cretan summer is long, hot, and dry, yet this little plant was going to live through it until the autumn rains arrived. It could do this because it grows from a bulb, and before the summer hit, it would retreat back to that bulb, hidden from the sun and needing no water.

What seemed so remarkable to me was how this miniscule flower was related to the showy bedding tulips I was used to seeing in parks and gardens. I saw other tulips on Crete that were larger and more brightly coloured, such as the pink-and-yellow *Tulipa saxatilis*, growing on the cliffs of a gorge or scattered through high-altitude meadows, but still they seemed remote from the garden tulips back home, which I found intriguing. I was beginning to fall for them.

Another turning point was a visit to Keukenhof in the Netherlands a few years later. This garden is devoted to bulbs, and in mid to late spring, it is the tulips that steal the show, and they really do put on a show. It is almost too much. There must be thousands and thousands of tulips all flowering at once. As you turn each corner, another stunning display confronts you. My experience at Keukenhof was the complete opposite of my encounter with the tiny tulip on Crete. Up to that point, I had been dismissive of tulips in bedding, but now I was well and truly hooked. This is how tulips should be grown and are grown in many gardens worldwide.

Bulbs are the perfect way for a plant to survive a long, dry summer, and they are easily transported when they are dormant, which is how tulips have found their way all over the world. Festivals, like those held in the Skagit Valley (United States) and Ottawa (Canada), celebrate the tulip with massed displays. The parks of Istanbul, where the craze for tulips has been reignited in recent years, are filled with millions of tulips every spring. In the United Kingdom, gardens devote space to tulips for their own festivals, bringing in visitors who marvel at the spectacle. Tulip festivals can be found across the globe from North America to South Korea, Japan, and Australia. Everyone, it seems, loves a tulip.

This love of tulips isn't new. The plants have been cultivated in Europe for well over 400 years, and before that they were celebrated in Constantinople (present-day Istanbul), in the days of the Ottoman Empire. It was the Dutch who perfected the cultivation and commercialization of the tulip once it had arrived from Turkey. They hybridized and selected tulips, producing new varieties by adding new species found in Central Asia into the mix. Carpets of bulbs now cover the flat fields of the Netherlands in spring, and the vast majority of tulips for sale today come from there.

Bedding isn't the only way to grow tulips, though. It is becoming more frequent to see them in mixed borders, growing alongside other spring perennials and bulbs or filling a gap before summer flowers bloom. More and more gardeners are growing tulips this way, notably in the Sussex garden of the late Christopher Lloyd, at Great Dixter in the United Kingdom. Here they are treated as border perennials, lifted for the summer but replanted in autumn to combine with a varied mix of spring flowers.

The dusky orange flower of *Tulipa orphanidea* Whittallii Group, from Turkey, one of my favourite tulip species

Tulips at Keukenhof

The huge flower and rich red colour of *Tulipa* 'World's Favourite', one of my favourite cultivars

Lily-flowered tulip 'Ballerina' along a path in the High Garden at Great Dixter

Whether you lift the bulbs for the summer or leave them in the ground, growing tulips as perennials rather than buying new bulbs every year leads to variation in their height and the size of the flower. The effect is more natural, if unpredictable, and I think that makes them even more appealing.

No other garden plant seems to arouse the passion that tulips do. It is hard to pinpoint the exact reason but the variation and continual reinventing of this glorious flower must play a part. The number of cultivars available can be daunting, but I want to give you some guidance by presenting a range of tulips in different colours, showing the various flower shapes, explaining the way the cultivars have been grouped together and, above all, providing the inspiration for you to try them yourself. You don't need a huge garden and you don't have to plant them in bedding; the different ways to grow tulips are as varied as the flowers themselves.

DESIGNING WITH TULIPS

B

Bright, *dazzling*, *impressive*, *imposing*, and *sumptuous*, even *dominating*—these are all words that can be used to describe the flowers of tulips. With names like 'Golden Parade', 'World's Favourite', 'Big Smile', and 'Olympic Flame', tulips are not expected to be shy and retiring. They burst upon the scene in early spring, reaching a crescendo by late spring before disappearing for the summer. They demand your attention and accommodating them in your garden will need some thought, otherwise what you imagined would be a joyous, flamboyant display might turn out to be overpowering, harsh, or even lurid.

If you do want to shock and surprise, then tulips are the right plant to use, but they can also be subtle and restrained. By combining complementary colours and planting among other ephemeral spring flowers, you can create a dreamy, harmonious scheme that's easy on the eye without sacrificing the wonderful colours tulips provide.

Thousands of tulip cultivars have been named over the years, and although most of them no longer exist or are not widely grown, a good bulb catalogue will still offer close to 200 different varieties. This means there is a huge range of possible combinations to try in your garden. The great thing about tulips is that if you don't like the effect you have created, you can dig up the bulbs and try something new the next year.

Tulips in bright primary colours can be harsh when planted together, but they can certainly dazzle when planted in dense blocks.

A mixture of pink and purple tulips creates a more harmonious scheme that still delivers plenty of colour.

Put very simply, there are three ways to use tulips in a garden. They can be planted as a bedding scheme, grown in containers, or incorporated into a garden border, mixed in with other permanent plants. Bedding is the most common way of growing tulips, especially in parks and large gardens. The bulbs are planted for their spring display and then dug up and replaced with summer-flowering plants. The following autumn, new bulbs are planted to create a different scheme. Most tulip cultivars are bred for bedding, and buying new bulbs every year ensures the uniformity of height and flower size that is essential for this style of planting. This is how amazing annual displays of tulips are made.

Tulips as Bedding Plants

The most dramatic use of the extravagant, vivid flowers of tulips is to plant them in large groups, packed together for a stunning display of colour. This is what modern tulips do best. Planting them in single cultivar groups or with other bulbs that flower at the same time results in a wonderful spring show, but before and after the tulips bloom, the ground will be bare.

This way of displaying tulips is used to great effect in gardens like Keukenhof, which is only open for a few weeks in spring so the appearance before and after is not important. However, more and more gardens are holding tulip festivals, where a part of the garden is set aside for the display. Borders filled with just tulips make an arresting sight and when the flowers are over, attention can turn to other parts of the garden.

The more traditional way to grow bedding is to mix the bulbs with plants that cover the bare ground and flower for a longer period. The bedding groundcover or carpet is planted in the autumn and the bulbs grow through them to flower in spring. Violas, polyanthus (*Primula*), double daisies (*Bellis*), and wallflowers (*Erysimum*) are typical of the plants grown with the bulbs. This type of planting is frequently used in municipal parks: one plant as edging, another to carpet the main area of the border, and the tulips growing through it. Although this tried-and-tested method can sometimes lack imagination, it is reliable and colourful. Done well, it can be fantastic but done badly it can end up looking dreary. The skill is in choosing the right tulips, mixing those that flower at the same time and in colours that complement each other.

At the end of spring, the bedding groundcover and bulbs are removed and replaced with summer bedding. The tulips are usually discarded, which seems a terrible waste, but unless they are stored in exactly the right conditions, many will have smaller flowers on shorter stems when they reappear the next spring or they may not flower at all.

A bedding display at the Royal Botanic Gardens, Kew, with white *Tulipa* 'Purissima' and purple 'Van der Neer'

A tulip festival at Cambo Estate in Scotland, with part of the garden devoted to tulips planted on their own. The display peaks in mid to late spring, with a range of colours and flower shapes that make an intoxicating scene.

A view of Keukenhof with banks of tulips and daffodils reaching down to the edge of a lake

Keukenhof

COVERING 32 HECTARES (79 acres), Keukenhof is a garden in Lisse, near Amsterdam, in the Netherlands. It is a showcase for over 7 million spring bulbs and only opens from March to May. Tulips are one of the highlights, especially from late April, and they are displayed in various combinations and styles of planting, all perfectly manicured. The result is stunning. There are formal beds, with tulips planted in blocks and lines, sometimes forming rivers of colour along with late daffodils, grape hyacinths (*Muscari*), and hyacinths. In some beds, different bulb mixes are displayed in less formal arrangements, demonstrating ideas you can try at home. Around lakes and under the trees, the beds of tulips seem never ending. You will need a whole day there and you will return full of inspiration. This is not the only way to grow tulips but it is certainly the most dramatic.

Triumph tulip 'Cairo' with the deep red
wallflower *Erysimum cheiri* 'Fire King'

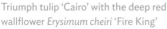

Tulipa 'Purissima' and *Primula* 'Crescendo Pink and Rose Shades'

The Dutch have perfected the environment in which the bulbs are stored over the summer to ensure they are in the best possible condition for flowering the following year. The buds are removed to help the bulb build up strength and once lifted the bulbs are stored dry and in the dark, at a temperature that is gradually decreased over the summer until they are ready to replant in autumn. Any fluctuations in temperature, especially in late summer, can cause the bulbs to divide once in the ground, leading to smaller, shorter plants.

In a more informal mixed border, variation in tulips is acceptable, even desirable, but if you want to create perfection in a bedding scheme, you just have to buy new bulbs every year. You can save bulbs from a bedding display and keep them cool and dry for the summer if you then plant them in a more relaxed part of the garden, where some tulips will settle down and flower for many years if the soil is fertile and well drained.

The exciting part of planting bedding is the design of the scheme and the chance to experiment with different colour associations every year. Some colours complement each other and others clash, but with tulips it doesn't always matter. Complementary colours create a more soothing effect, but clashing colours often provide greater impact and an element of surprise.

Growing tulips along with other spring-flowering bulbs can extend the period of bloom and the choice of colours available. No tulips are true blue so the addition of a

The Lily-flowered tulip 'China Pink' growing through *Myosotis* 'Dwarf Indigo'

The yellow flowers of *Tulipa* 'West Point' and *Narcissus* 'Hawera' combine beautifully with the blue of *Muscari*, *Ipheion*, and *Anemone blanda*.

Single Late tulip 'Bleu Aimable' growing through forget-me-not (*Myosotis*) at Great Dixter

Triumph tulips 'Shirley' and 'Purple Prince' in a formal garden, growing beside a low box hedge

This predominantly yellow-and-white scheme is given some punch by a few blooms of the pink Single Early tulip 'Beauty Queen'. The yellow *Narcissus* 'Little Witch' and white *N.* 'Jack Snipe' flower at the same time as early to mid-season tulips like the pale sulphur yellow Fosteriana tulip 'Concerto'.

Triumph tulips 'New Design' and the dark purple 'Negrita' form a pleasing combination. The white in the flower of 'New Design', as well as the remaining blooms of *Narcissus* 'Trena', gives the scheme a lift and contrasts with the more sombre note of 'Negrita'.

White tulips go with any other colour, in this case the deep orange of 'Orange Emperor'. This creates a bright and uplifting display.

A warm display of the complementary colours orange, red, and pale yellow. The Fosteriana tulip 'Orange Emperor' and bright red Darwin Hybrid 'Parade' go well with the orange-cupped daffodil *Narcissus* 'Altruist'. The pale petals of the daffodil make this colour scheme work, as well as the underplanting of white anemones. Without the lighter note, the scheme would be too intense.

Another example of two complementary colours, this time the bright reddish pink Darwin Hybrid 'Van Eijk' and the darker Triumph tulip 'Jumbo Pink'. However, without a pale flower mixed in, the richness of the colours is a little overpowering.

The yellow Lily-flowered tulip 'West Point' planted in a block along-side box hedges cut into cubes to form a more contemporary look.

A collection of tulips in containers can bring vibrant colour to the garden in spring without the need to plant in borders or create a bedding scheme.

Most of the tulips in this scene are white, but the impact of the red tulips shows how dominant the colour red can be. Both are Triumph tulips, called 'White Love' and 'Red Love'. A display like this will be short lived, as there are no other bulbs or bedding plants to extend the period of bloom.

bulb like hyacinth (*Hyacinthus*) or grape hyacinth (*Muscari*) can provide the blue needed to complement a yellow tulip like 'West Point'. Blue-flowered Grecian wind-flower (*Anemone blanda*) or spring starflower (*Ipheion uniflorum*) can also provide that blue backdrop and a white, like *Anemone* 'White Splendour', can make a suitable background for any colour.

Let's be realistic though. Unless you have a huge garden or love bedding so much that you devote every inch to these regimented displays, you are unlikely to grow tulips on a large scale in the traditional bedding style. On a domestic scale, you are more likely to plant tulips among permanent plants, under trees and shrubs, along the foot of a hedge, or beside a path where they grow with herbaceous perennials. I think tulips look great with low hedges of box or yew, which is reminiscent of how tulips may have been grown in an eighteenth-century garden. You can still lift the bulbs every summer to give them a dry dormant season before replanting in autumn, but if you like a level of uniformity, then it is best to plant new bulbs every year.

A dazzling display of tulips and other bulbs in containers at Great Dixter

Tulips in Containers

If you don't want to plant bedding or you haven't the room, then there is an alternative way to bring the splendour of tulips into your garden. Tulips are perfect for growing in containers; it's like portable bedding. Bring them out when in flower, hide them away when they're done, or remove the bulbs once they have died down and use the same container for summer plants.

Any tulip can be grown in a container, but the shorter-stemmed cultivars look best and are more resilient in the wind. You can use tall-stemmed tulips but think about the size of container and keep it in proportion with the tulips.

I usually prefer just one cultivar in a pot, but you can combine different tulips, especially if you use a large container. If there is a colour combination you want to create, make sure the cultivars you choose will flower at the same time. Choosing two cultivars from the same cultivar group, like Triumph, Parrot, or Single Late tulips, will normally ensure they flower simultaneously. If you mix an early tulip, like a Kaufmanniana, and a late-flowering cultivar, like a Fringed tulip, in one container, when the second tulip is in bloom the first will have faded petals and possibly browning leaves, so bear that in mind.

You can also plant other bulbs in the same container that either flower with the tulips or appear earlier to add a bit of colour before the tulips open. Crocus flower in late winter and their relatively narrow leaves will not spoil the display once the tulips are out. In fact, the later tulip leaves will probably hide the crocus foliage from view. *Muscari* and *Anemone blanda* are used to great effect as a backdrop to tulips in bedding displays and the same effect can be created in a container. Other flowers that appear at the same time include the later daffodils like *Narcissus* 'Hawera', 'Jack Snipe', and 'Quail', to name just a few. You can also use more traditional bedding plants to fill the pot, like pansies or polyanthus, or you could use forget-me-not (*Myosotis*), the leaves of coralbell (*Heuchera*), or sedge (*Carex*), or anything that provides a suitable backdrop to the tulip's bloom. Just remember that the tulip is the flower everyone will be looking at.

Triumph tulips 'Shirley' and 'Purple Prince' in an old water trough at Wakehurst Place in Sussex, United Kingdom

A miniature bedding scheme in a pot, with Lily-flowered tulip 'Pretty Woman', the dark maroon leaves of *Heuchera*, and blue violas

A container of the white Lily-flowered tulip 'Très Chic' planted with forget-me-not (*Myosotis*) and a pot of Triumph tulip 'Tropical Dream' in the background

A pot planted up with Greigii tulip 'Cape Cod'

Great Dixter

THE GREAT GARDENER, plantsman, and writer, the late Christopher Lloyd (1921–2006), gardened at Great Dixter, in East Sussex, United Kingdom, for most of his life. He was passionate about plants and devised inspiring combinations, which he tried out in his garden. Head Gardener Fergus Garrett has continued and developed this style of planting, and tulips are among the wonderful spring displays that you can see here. In containers around the house and borders throughout the garden, tulips are grown among a range of other plants. The bulbs in the borders are mostly lifted for the summer, sorted, stored, and replanted, with new additions to ensure a perfect display. This must be the best garden to visit in Britain to gain ideas and inspiration for planting tulips in a mixed border.

Lily-flowered tulip 'Red Shine' in the Long Border at Great Dixter

A mixture of pink and purple tulips pushing through spring pea (*Lathyrus vernus*) and blue and white forms of Siberian bugloss (*Brunnera macrophylla*)

Viridiflora tulip 'Spring Green' and Lily-flowered 'Ballade' in the Walled Garden at Great Dixter

Tulips in Mixed Borders

This is where it gets interesting. For a dramatic contrast to angular blocks of formal bedding, you can scatter tulips through a border, mingling them with other plants and forming irregular clusters that merge into each other. You can still grow them like bedding, by planting new bulbs every year, but the effect is much more informal, and if done well, the tulips can even look like they have naturally appeared, pushing through the foliage and peering out from the shadows to make the most of the spring sunshine. Some tulips will survive left in the ground and the variation in size and height that will inevitably occur only reinforces the image of a natural colony that has chosen your garden as its home.

Planting tulips in an established herbaceous border, around shrubs or under trees, or designing a new planting scheme that mixes tulips with permanent plants, can open up a whole range of possibilities. How long a tulip will survive left in the ground depends on the soil, climate, and the cultivar.

A Mediterranean-type climate, which naturally has dry summers, is more like the conditions found where wild tulips grow, but where summer rain is normal, you may have more success by digging up the dormant bulbs to keep them dry. However, cultivated tulips are remarkably adaptable and many will be fine left in the ground if drainage is good. Certain cultivar groups are more likely to include tulips that do well if left to naturalize in the garden and many tulip species are especially persistent in the garden, as long as they have that well-drained soil.

The cultivar groups (discussed elsewhere) that clearly show evidence of tulip species in their makeup are generally more adaptable to garden conditions. These include the Kaufmanniana, Greigii, and Fosteriana tulips. The influence of *Tulipa fosteriana* is also apparent in the Darwin Hybrids, which often do well if planted permanently. Those in groups like Single Early, Triumph, Fringed, Parrot, and Single Late are less likely to keep flowering if left in the ground so are best stored dry for the summer and replanted in autumn, although there are always exceptions and a lot depends on the conditions in which they are grown.

The Darwin Hybrid tulip 'Daydream' in the Peacock Garden at Great Dixter, growing through the leaves of lupins, with forget-me-not (*Myosotis*) and white honesty (*Lunaria annua*)

Tulips along a flagstone path at Great Dixter

The Kaufmanniana tulip 'Love Song' planted with yellow-flowered *Epimedium pinnatum* subsp. *colchicum*

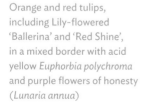

Orange and red tulips, including Lily-flowered 'Ballerina' and 'Red Shine', in a mixed border with acid yellow *Euphorbia polychroma* and purple flowers of honesty (*Lunaria annua*)

COMPANION PLANTS AND SUPPORT ACTS

Some beautiful plant combinations can be created by growing tulips in a border with other plants that flower at the same time. These may be bulbs, like the later-flowering daffodils (*Narcissus*) or spring perennials, such as *Brunnera*, bleeding heart (*Dicentra*), *Pulmonaria*, spurge (*Euphorbia*), or *Epimedium*. These companion plants can be chosen to provide a colour that complements the tulip.

The delicate yellow flowers of *Epimedium pinnatum* or *E.* 'Sulphureum' are usually associated with shady conditions, but they do well in dappled shade under deciduous trees and this also suits tulips, which will bloom while the trees are bare and still letting sunlight through to the ground below. A billowing carpet of *Epimedium* will form a backdrop to the orange blooms of a tulip like 'Love Song' or 'Orange Emperor'.

The spring flowers of *Pulmonaria*, *Brunnera*, and forget-me-not (*Myosotis*) provide the blue to go with pink, yellow, or white tulips. Early spurges like *Euphorbia polychroma* or the grey-leaved, sun-loving *E. myrsinites* will flower alongside tulips. The lime green and acid yellow flower heads of the spurges contrast with the rich colours of tulips such as 'Queen of Night', 'Burgundy', or 'Red Shine'.

Even without flowers, the new shoots and fresh young foliage of herbaceous perennials such as hardy geraniums, lupins, peonies (*Paeonia*), and oriental poppies (*Papaver orientale*) provide a backdrop to the tulip's blooms that varies in colour and texture. Peony shoots are often tinted red or purple when young, oriental poppies have a rough, hairy surface, and geraniums and lupins form mounds of delicate, airy foliage that erupts from

The Greigii tulip 'Ali Baba' growing through the spotted foliage and blue flowers of *Pulmonaria* and the ferny leaves of *Dicentra formosa*

the ground before they flower later in the spring or early summer. The ever-changing, burgeoning floral landscape of the border is enhanced and brightened by tulips, which add some early colour before these perennials flower. They can transform what might otherwise be a forgotten corner of the garden and will have died down by the time the herbaceous plants bloom. The space left by the tulips will then be filled with bountiful summer colour.

The best effect is created if the bulbs are not spaced too thinly. Plant clusters of tulips that become more dispersed as they gently spread through the border. Mix different but complementary colours: pinks with purples, yellow with orange. Plant the tulips at the foot of a hedge or wall. The warm terracotta colour of a brick wall makes a great background to red or yellow flowers. A dark hedge or the purple foliage of shrubs like *Pittosporum tenuifolium* 'Tom Thumb' help bright tulips stand out. For stark contrast, plant tulips to grow through the black leaves of *Ophiopogon planiscapus* 'Nigrescens' or a dark-leaved bugle, such as of *Ajuga reptans* 'Atropurpurea' or 'Braunherz'. The background and surrounding plants are important to consider, as they provide the stage for the tulips' brief spell in the limelight.

Lily-flowered tulip 'Moonshine' growing through *Bergenia* and the black leaves of *Ophiopogon planiscapus* 'Nigrescens', with a scattering of white wood anemone (*Anemone nemorosa*)

Tulipa orphanidea Whittallii Group and 'China Pink' growing through the dark leaves of *Ajuga reptans* 'Braunherz' in a narrow border, with *Phormium* as a backdrop

The Single Early tulip 'Ruby Red' with *Narcissus* 'Ambergate' and the new, red-tinted leaves of peony.

Triumph tulip 'Abu Hassan' providing colour in a border before summer flowers bloom

Single Early tulips 'Candy Prince' and 'Purple Prince' brighten a mixed border at Wakehurst Place.

GRAVEL GARDENS

Gravel gardens have become increasingly popular in recent years, created with the aim of reducing irrigation to a minimum or not watering the plants at all. The only moisture for the plants comes from natural precipitation so those that are grown successfully are drought tolerant and able to cope with dry conditions for an extended period. The ground is free draining, as these plants do not like heavy, wet soil, and is covered with a thick mulch of gravel. This mulch keeps wet soil away from the leaves, as well as keeping down weeds and conserving what moisture there is in the soil. A gravel garden is perfect for tulips.

Tulips like 'Couleur Cardinal', 'Love Song', 'West Point', and 'Burgundy', and species like *Tulipa turkestanica* and *T. orphanidea* Whittallii Group can be planted in a gravel garden and left to flower for several years. Many drought-tolerant plants have grey foliage and these complement the tulips' colourful blooms. *Salvia*, *Phlomis*, *Lavandula*, *Stachys*, *Teucrium*, and bearded irises are among the plants that do well in gravel garden conditions and their leaves form a muted backdrop to the tulips.

Lily-flowered tulip 'Burgundy' growing through thick gravel mulch

Triumph tulip 'Couleur Cardinal' growing with grey-leaved plants in a gravel garden, including a small *Hebe* and the new shoots of *Perovskia*

Tulips for a Gravel Garden

Tulipa 'Burgundy'
Tulipa 'China Pink'
Tulipa clusiana 'Lady Jane'
Tulipa 'Couleur Cardinal'
Tulipa 'Honky Tonk'
Tulipa 'Love Song'
Tulipa 'Madame Lefeber'
Tulipa 'Orange Emperor'
Tulipa 'Spring Green'
Tulipa turkestanica
Tulipa 'West Point'

Tulipa linifolia planted between large rocks at the Royal Botanic Gardens, Kew

ROCK GARDENS

A rock garden provides even better drainage than a gravel garden by raising the soil above ground level. A mulch of gravel does the same job as in a gravel garden, keeping the leaves dry and suppressing weeds. The rocks themselves evoke images of a tulip's natural habitat, on rocky slopes in the hills and mountains of southern Europe and Asia. This is one reason why tulip species are particularly well suited to a rock garden. Their smaller size is in scale with the other mountain plants they grow with and the free-draining soil ensures that some species can survive for many years without the need to lift the bulbs.

The varied aspects and features of a rock garden offer a selection of different niches for growing tulips. Gaps between the rocks are like natural crevices, and bulbs can be planted so it appears the tulip is emerging from the rock. Sunny slopes and partially shaded gullies provide different conditions for plants to grow, and a number of tulips can be grown successfully outside in these types of location. Some of the most reliable include *Tulipa linifolia*, *T. tarda*, *T. saxatilis* and its selection 'Lilac Wonder', *T. praestans* 'Fusilier', and *T. orphanidea* Whittallii Group. Where there is a little more moisture in the soil or partial shade from the surrounding rocks, try *T. sylvestris*, *T. clusiana*, or *T. humilis* and the hybrids 'Little Princess' and 'Little Beauty'.

A sunny slope converted into a small rock garden, with a range of spring plants growing through the gravel mulch, including tulips, *Primula*, *Muscari*, and pasque flowers (*Anemone*)

Red-flowered *Tulipa linifolia* (left) and purplish *T.* 'Little Beauty' (right), growing with primroses (*Primula vulgaris*), *Muscari*, and the tiny spurge *Euphorbia cyparissias*

Not all gardens are large enough to accommodate a significant rock garden, but the principles of rock gardening can be applied in the domestic garden. All you need is a sunny slope and you can convert it into a small garden border with gravel mulch and a few rocks to provide the right conditions for a range of smaller tulips. For a more formal or contemporary design, a raised bed will perform the same function, increasing drainage and lifting the plants nearer to eye level, where you can enjoy those delicate-looking blooms of the tulip species or smaller cultivars.

A raised bed can be constructed out of a range of materials, from wooden railway sleepers or brick to the more rustic dry stone wall. In a contemporary garden design, white rendered walls may be used to form angular beds around a terrace or lawn. These can be treated like large containers, with the bulbs lifted every year and replaced with a new design the following autumn. Plant these beds with the Lily-flowered tulip 'White Triumphator' backed with clipped box, or mix in the dark purple 'Queen of Night' for a sophisticated, minimalist display. Raised beds can be incorporated into any garden design and the inclusion of tulips will bring light and colour to the planting scheme.

Tulips for a Rock Garden

A ROCK GARDEN is perfect for the smaller species and this list includes those that are among the most reliable. They will also do well in a raised bed, as long as they are not swamped by surrounding plants.

Tulipa aucheriana
Tulipa clusiana
Tulipa dasystemon
Tulipa humilis

Tulipa kaufmanniana
Tulipa linifolia and cultivars
Tulipa 'Little Beauty'
Tulipa 'Little Princess'
Tulipa orphanidea and cultivars
Tulipa praestans 'Fusilier'
Tulipa saxatilis 'Lilac Wonder'
Tulipa tarda
Tulipa sylvestris

Tulipa saxatilis in full sun on the rock garden at the Royal Botanic Gardens, Kew

The bright red *Tulipa sprengeri* flowering with *Maianthemum racemosum* in a woodland garden border at Kew

WOODLAND GARDENS

A woodland garden may not seem the obvious place to grow tulips. Shade and moisture in the soil are not what tulips need, but in winter and early spring, deciduous trees allow plenty of light through to the woodland floor when the tulips are in growth. Then, as the tulips die down for the summer, the leaves on the trees unfurl and soon they are sucking all the moisture out of the ground. Without irrigation and the addition of organic matter, the soil beneath trees can become very dry in summer, which is just how tulips like it.

Not all tulips will do well in a woodland garden as the soil tends to be humus-rich and moisture-retentive as a result of being cultivated to accommodate a wide range of shade-tolerant plants, but some tulips can thrive in this situation, as long as they are not kept too shaded or too wet. The best of these is *Tulipa sprengeri*. This wonderful scarlet tulip thrives in soil that doesn't dry out completely in summer. It can be scattered through a semi-shaded woodland border, where it will emerge alongside the new foliage of ferns and hostas and bloom with plants like false Solomon's seal (*Maianthemum racemosum*). It also produces plenty of seed, which will sow itself around the parent plant and germinate, to gradually form a spreading colony.

In drier soil under trees, some of the Fosteriana and Darwin Hybrid tulips will also do well. Cultivars like 'Golden Parade', 'Yellow Purissima', and 'Apeldoorn' will bloom in mid-spring, taking over from earlier daffodils. I have found some Lily-flowered tulips like 'China Pink' and 'Moonshine' do well in this type of situation. A group of tulips that have been given species names, known as neo-tulips, are also well suited to more humus-rich soil. These tulips have escaped from cultivation in the Alps, particularly the Savoy region of France. Exactly how they got there is not known, but they have become naturalized in the countryside, probably hybridizing and looking very like wild species. Some are available to buy, such as *T. saracenica*, *T. marjoletii*, and *T. mauritiana*, and are worth planting in the dappled shade under trees or in the partial shade of an east-or west-facing wall. Plant them beneath a flowering cherry and the blossom will open at the same time as these mid-season tulips.

Yellow-flowered *Tulipa marjoletii* in a partially shaded border with the dark blue perennial cornflower (*Centaurea montana*)

Tulips for Woodland Gardens

THESE ARE JUST a few of the tulips that I know from experience do well in dappled shade under deciduous trees. There will be many more, especially those from the same cultivar groups as those listed here.

Tulipa clusiana
Tulipa 'Daydream'
Tulipa 'Golden Parade'
Tulipa humilis
Tulipa marjoletti

Tulipa mauritiana
Tulipa 'Orange Emperor'
Tulipa saracenica
Tulipa sprengeri

Tulipa 'Golden Parade' growing under trees and bringing a splash of colour to an otherwise bare border

GRASSY MEADOWS

Tulips are rarely grown in grass, mainly because by the time the tulip leaves have died down, the grass has become long and untidy. Cutting the grass too early in the season will also cut off the tulip leaves while still green, weakening the plant and possibly killing it. You would have to treat the area as a meadow.

The other disadvantage is that it is harder to lift bulbs once planted under grass, so only tulips that can be relied upon to return every spring should be grown in this way. But if you have a patch of long grass, maybe with wildflowers that you leave until summer to cut back, then there are a few tulips that can add to the spring colour.

Tulipa sprengeri is apparently suited to growing in grass, although I have never tried it. If the soil gets very dry in summer it may not do so well, but some Fosteriana tulips such as 'Madame Lefeber' and 'Orange Emperor' can survive these conditions. I have grown the latter in a neglected, overgrown corner of the garden for over a decade and it still flowers, peering through the grass stems.

It just goes to show that there are no fixed rules with tulips. There are always exceptions, and the variety of garden situations in which you can grow tulips is far from limited. Yes, they are mainly grown for bedding and containers, but experimenting with them in a mixed, informal border, under trees and shrubs, or even in grass is well worth the effort. Only by trying different cultivars and colour combinations will you find out what works best in your garden, and which tulips make the most pleasing display.

Tulipa 'Orange Emperor' growing among the pale brown stems of long grass

A variegated grass is the perfect foil for *Tulipa* 'Mickey Mouse'.

UNDER-
STANDING
TULIPS

T

Tulips are often associated with Turkey because it is from there that they were brought into Europe in the sixteenth century. Most tulip species are from further east, in the rocky valleys, hills, and mountains of Central Asia but, because of their intensely colourful flowers, they were grown and revered in Turkey, especially in Constantinople (present-day Istanbul), the capital of the Ottoman Empire. There, tulips with long narrow, pointed petals—often called needle tulips—were especially favoured.

From Turkey, the cultivated tulip spread west and began to be grown in gardens, particularly in central and northern Europe, including Austria, France, Germany, Belgium, and the Netherlands. Old paintings and drawings of seventeenth- and eighteenth-century European gardens usually show tulips as individual plants, evenly spaced apart or lined up in a border. They were grown as specimens to be enjoyed in their own right and this was especially true in the Netherlands in the 1630s, at the height of Tulipomania.

The Dutch craze for tulips at that time was fed by the mystery surrounding so-called broken tulips, in which the colour in the flower was split into a pattern of feathers and flames over a pale background of white or yellow. How a plain-coloured tulip, which was called a breeder, changed in one year to a broken tulip was unknown at the time, and it

Tulipa acuminata is a remarkable tulip with exquisitely narrow, sinuous petals that form a pointed flower reminiscent of the exotic-looking needle tulips so popular in the Ottoman Empire.

was the best and rarest broken tulips that commanded the highest prices. Tulip bulbs were bought and sold like shares on the stock market, the owners probably never actually seeing the plant before selling it on for a profit.

This madness for tulips led to astronomical prices for individual bulbs until, in 1637, the market collapsed, leaving some unlucky traders with massive debts. Although there must have been many people who never wanted to see a tulip again after 1637, for those that saw tulips as beautiful garden plants rather than a commodity, the passion for them never wavered.

With tulips, it's all about the flower.

The cause of the broken tulips is now known to be a virus, called the tulip breaking virus or TBV. The virus is spread by aphids and in this way can infect a breeder tulip, leading to the broken colours and delicate patterning. In the United Kingdom, these broken tulips were known as Florists' tulips and in the nineteenth century were exhibited at flower shows held in public houses, the cut blooms displayed in brown beer bottles. Today the Wakefield and North of England Tulip Society is the last surviving UK tulip society and holds a show every year, the revered blooms still exhibited in beer bottles.

In the late nineteenth century, broken tulips remained the focus of attention. They were grown in gardens, sometimes under a cumbersome framework that held a canvas screen to protect the flowers. Under this canvas, tulips were grown, often in two parallel beds with a path down the centre, the bulbs planted in rows on either side. It may have been unsightly but this type of structure was necessary for protecting the flowers from heavy rain and hail. The main reason for growing them was to exhibit the blooms, so keeping them pristine was essential.

In the 1880s, attention turned to the breeder tulips as worthy garden plants in their own right. These plain-coloured varieties, which were mainly grown in the hope that they would break, were bedded out in the garden not for their display value, but in case they turned into a wonderful new variety. However, in 1889 Dutch grower E. H. Krelage planted a display of tall, late-flowering breeder tulips at the Great Exhibition in Paris and called them Darwin tulips. His bedding display of massed flowers caught the public's imagination. Tulip growers began to look for more breeders to use, such as the Cottage tulips, so-called because they were usually discarded breeders that survived in cottage gardens.

Then, with the introduction of new species, such as *Tulipa fosteriana*, the development of new and varied tulip cultivars gained momentum and the craze for bedding led to mass plantings of tulips to create displays that are ever more spectacular. The Dutch led the way in the breeding of new cultivars and they are great salespeople, creating a product that needs replacing every year to maintain the intended effect. The Netherlands is still the centre of tulip breeding, growing, and trading. A springtime trip to Amsterdam wouldn't be complete without a tour of the bulb fields to see the dramatic rows of colourful tulips.

Tulip flowers grab your attention, like this Lily-flowered 'China Pink', catching the sunlight on a spring morning

The leaves of *Tulipa greigii* showing characteristic dark anthocyanin markings

The Plant

With tulips, it's all about the flower. Leaves have a part to play, of course, but they are the support act, providing a backdrop to the colourful blooms. The size and form of the flower, as well as flowering time, are used to place cultivated tulips into one of 15 groups. By choosing to grow tulips from different groups, you can extend the period of flowering and have a variety of flower shapes on display.

Some tulip foliage is quite attractive, especially those leaves that have dark dashes and stripes, caused by anthocyanin pigment, the same pigment that gives red tulip flowers their colour. Leaves may be wide with a rounded tip or long, narrow, and pointed. They are often grey-green or blue-green, but some are bright green and glossy. The leaves are held on the flower stem and are usually crowded towards the base. The stem itself grows out the top of the bulb, which is buried below ground.

The bulb is where it all begins. It is an adaptation made by wild tulips to survive a long period of drought in summer. Many tulip species grow in the hills and mountains of countries like Iran, Uzbekistan, Kyrgyzstan, and Kazakhstan, where the summer is long, hot, and dry. This is when the tulip plant is dormant. The bulb is an underground storage organ, made from swollen leaf bases surrounding a bud that will develop into the stem, leaves, and flower once the autumn rains bring the tulip back to life after its summer rest.

A stolon growing from the bulb of *Tulipa saxatilis*

The brown outer layer of the bulb is often brittle or leathery and is called the tunic. Beneath the tunic is the firm, creamy white flesh of the bulb and at its base is a small area called the basal plate, from which the new roots grow. Unusually for a bulbous plant, a tulip grows a new bulb every year. Most other bulbs just get bigger, with a new layer added each year, but the tulip uses all its food reserves to grow a new plant and then produces a new bulb before the leaves and stem die back in early summer. This is important for gardeners to know because if the plant is allowed to dry out when in full growth or the leaves are cut back too soon, it will not have a chance to build up a healthy, strong new bulb that will flower the following spring.

In some years, a healthy single tulip bulb will be replaced by three or four new bulbs, with only one of flowering size and the others taking a few years to build up the strength to bloom. This is one way tulips increase vegetatively. The other way is by producing stolons, which are growths that extend from the bulb underground to produce a new bulb a short distance from the mother plant. This is usually seen in some of the wild species, like *Tulipa saxatilis*, rather than in the garden cultivars, and it enables a tulip to spread naturally without having to flower. In this way, the yellow-flowered *T. sylvestris* has spread north from its natural habitat in southern Europe to reach as far as the United Kingdom and southern Scandinavia. It often doesn't flower unless the preceding summer was warm and relatively dry but it will still produce leaves and spread underground by its stolons. The other way tulips increase naturally is by producing seed, and to do that they need to flower.

Most tulips have just one flower but a few are multi-flowered, with a branched stem holding several buds. Three or four buds are normal for multi-flowered tulips but some species, like *Tulipa turkestanica*, can have up to 12 flowers from one bulb (see photo on page 144). The flower is composed of six petals or, more correctly, perianth segments, also known as tepals. Perianth segments are the petals and sepals, and in many flowers, the sepals are green and enclose the bud, protecting the flower before it opens. In a tulip flower, the perianth segments are all brightly coloured and there is no distinction between petals and sepals. However, in common language they are usually referred to as petals and that is what I call them below and in the tulip descriptions.

The six petals in a tulip flower are arranged into two whorls of three. The three inner petals are often a slightly different shape than the outer three and are sometimes held more upright as the flower opens. They surround the six pollen-producing anthers and the central ovary, topped by the stigma. The base of the petals may be a different colour to the rest of the flower, creating what is usually referred to as the "blotch." The blotch may be white or yellow but is more frequently dark, such as a deep olive green or bluish black, and it may have a narrow yellow margin. It is well worth looking inside the flower to see the various markings that you might otherwise miss.

Tulips with Variegated Foliage

Tulipa 'Fire of Love'
Tulipa 'Jaap Groot'
Tulipa 'New Design'
Tulipa praestans 'Unicum'
Tulipa 'Purissima Design'

The flower of the Triumph tulip 'Tropical Dream' showing two whorls of petals, the six anthers around the pale yellow stigma of the ovary, and the dark central blotch

Tulipa sylvestris has spread purely by stolons through parts of northern Europe and makes a good garden plant.

Single Early tulip 'Christmas Marvel'

Single Early tulip 'Apricot Beauty'

Cultivar Groups

Since the first tulips were introduced to cultivation in Europe, they have been crossed with each other and new forms selected to produce the thousands of cultivars that have been registered today. As new species were discovered and introduced into cultivation—*Tulipa greigii* and *T. kaufmanniana* in the 1870s and *T. fosteriana* early in the twentieth century—they were used to breed additional new cultivars by crossing with existing garden tulips. Many cultivars are sports, which are variations that arise spontaneously, growing from offsets of the parent bulb. These sports will flower at the same time as the parent plant, but they are usually a different colour or combination of colours.

The 15 cultivar groups used to classify tulips today range from the early flowering tulips with single flowers on short stems to the tall, late, double-flowered cultivars. Some have long, pointed petals while others have a chopped fringe along the petal margins. Three of the groups are named after the species *T. kaufmanniana*, *T. greigii*, and *T. fosteriana* and consist of the cultivars that most closely resemble those species. The last group is called Miscellaneous and includes all the tulip species and hybrids that don't fit in one of the other groups.

Double Early 'Verona'

SINGLE EARLY GROUP

These are not the earliest tulips to flower but they do start to bloom in the first half of spring. They have a single, neat, cup-shaped flower, held on a short, sturdy stem, typically around 35 cm (14 inches) tall. This is not a large group of cultivars but it includes a few well-known tulips, like 'Apricot Beauty' and 'Christmas Dream', which is a sport of 'Christmas Marvel'. Single Early tulips make good container plants, their strong stems holding up well in the wind.

DOUBLE EARLY GROUP

The double flowers of these tulips are an unruly cluster of petals held at the end of a short stem. They form wide, colourful flowers that don't need the sun to open up and make an impression. Flowering in early to mid-spring, they have a stem that is typically 25–30 cm (10–12 inches) tall, although it can reach 45 cm (18 inches) in some cultivars. One of the oldest tulips in this group is 'Murillo', which dates from 1860 and has given rise to a large number of sports that come in a range of colours. As well as the more colourful cultivars, there are some beautiful creamy white and pale yellow tulips in this group, like 'Verona' and 'Montreux'.

Triumph tulip 'Couleur Cardinal' with
bicolored Double Early 'Monsella'

Triumph tulip 'Passionale'

TRIUMPH GROUP

Sometime called mid-season tulips, this is one of the largest groups of tulips, consisting of a number of well-known and popular cultivars, such as 'Shirley', 'Prinses Irene', and the wonderful 'Couleur Cardinal', which dates from 1845 and is still available today. The flowers are similar to those in the Single Early Group but they tend to have slightly taller stems, typically 35–50 cm (14–20 inches) tall, and bloom a little later, in mid-spring. These tulips were originally a result of crossing Single Early tulips with the old Darwin Group tulips (now grouped with the Single Late tulips).

DARWIN HYBRID GROUP

If you want large-flowered tulips, then the Darwin Hybrids are the tulips to choose. Great bowls open almost flat in the sun and come in a range of rich and vibrant colours. The stem is typically around 55 cm (22 inches) tall but is sturdy. The mid-season flowers, with their large, wide petals, can be susceptible to windy, wet weather. This group was originally the result of crossing the late-flowering Darwin tulips with species like *Tulipa fosteriana*, from which they have inherited the large flower. *Tulipa fosteriana* has also given the Darwin Hybrids their habit of persisting in the garden and they can last a few years without lifting the bulbs if the soil conditions are right. 'Apeldoorn' is one of the classic tulips in the group and has several sports. Developments that are more recent include the Impression series, with huge bright flowers, such as 'Red Impression'.

Darwin Hybrid tulip 'World's Favourite'

Darwin Hybrid tulips 'Pink Impression' and 'Red Impression'

SINGLE LATE GROUP

This large and popular group of single tulips flowers late in the spring with an egg-shaped bud that opens to a rounded cup-shaped bloom. Sometimes called May-flowering tulips, the plants have a tall stem that can reach 60–70 cm (24–28 inches) tall or more, and they are widely used in bedding, providing an impressive and colourful end to the tulip season. The group was formed in 1981 by merging the old Darwin and Cottage groups. Single Late tulips can be planted in a mixed border but often do not last long unless the bulbs are lifted in summer. There are exceptions, with some old Cottage tulips surviving outside for several years. This group includes the wonderful, dark 'Queen of Night' but also more subtle pastel shades, such as pale orange and rose 'Dordogne', salmon pink 'Menton', and pinkish red 'Avignon'.

Single Late
tulip 'Avignon'

Single Late tulips 'Maureen' (white) and 'Menton' (salmon pink)

Lily-flowered tulip 'Fly Away'

Lily-flowered tulip 'Pieter de Leur'

LILY-FLOWERED GROUP

The elegant tulips in this group have elongated, pointed petals that make a goblet-shaped bloom, narrowing above the base to form a waist below the flaring tips. As the flower opens, the petals arch back. The stems vary from 25 to 60 cm (10 to 24 inches) tall and the flowers open in mid to late spring. These tulips were originally bred from the old Darwin and Cottage tulips and the group was formed in 1958. Some members of this group have long, narrow petals, like the dark purple 'Burgundy', while others have a more restrained form but still retain that curvaceous profile, such as 'Red Shine', 'China Pink', and the lovely orange and red 'Ballerina'.

FRINGED GROUP

The petal margins of this unusual and distinctive group of tulips are cut into small triangular teeth that look especially crystalline when the margin is a paler colour than the rest of the flower, as in the cultivars 'Cummins' and 'Talitha'. The bulbs flower in mid to late spring, on stems of variable length but typically around 55 cm (22 inches) tall. These frilly tulips are not to everyone's taste and they look better in bedding or a container than in a more informal setting but some, like the deep pink 'Louvre' and the rich purple 'Cuban Night', are quite striking.

Fringed tulip 'Honeymoon'

Fringed tulip 'Talitha'

Viridiflora tulip 'Red Spring Green'

Viridiflora tulip 'Flaming Spring Green'

VIRIDIFLORA GROUP

The tulips in this group all have green markings on the flower, normally as a green wash or flame reaching up the centre of each petal from the base. The single flowers open in mid to late spring and are held on a stem of variable height but most are around 50 cm (20 inches) tall. The best known in the group is the popular 'Spring Green' but newer cultivars include 'Red Spring Green' and 'Flaming Spring Green'.

REMBRANDT GROUP

This group was created for tulips infected with the tulip breaking virus (TBV). They resemble tulips seen in seventeenth-century Dutch still life paintings or the old English Florists' tulips. The virus, which causes the flower colour to become streaked or broken with a pattern of feathers or flames over the base colour, is spread by aphids and can easily be transferred to other plants like lilies, as well as other tulips. For this reason, true Rembrandt tulips are not offered commercially but they do survive in historical collections, and in England, members of the Wakefield and North of England Tulip Society still grow and exhibit the English Florists' tulips. Today you can buy bulbs listed as Rembrandt tulips but they are stable cultivars. They are not infected with TBV but have flames and feathers on the petals that make them look similar to infected flowers. Tulips sometimes sold as Rembrandts include 'Olympic Flame', 'Flaming Spring Green', and even 'Shirley' but these all belong to other groups.

The variegated flower of a modern tulip in the Rembrandt Group is stable, unlike the broken tulips of old whose flames and feathers were the result of a virus.

Parrot tulip 'Black Parrot'

Parrot tulip 'Bright Parrot'

PARROT GROUP

The bizarre but fascinating tulips in this group have their petals cut and twisted along the margins. Some of them have contorted petals with flashes of green or yellow over a darker background, like 'Rococo', a sport of the Triumph tulip 'Couleur Cardinal'. They range from the slightly grotesque pink-and-green 'Green Wave' to the more subtle 'Apricot Parrot', which has white flowers feathered with pale pink, and they include the dark purple 'Black Parrot' and violet-purple 'Blue Parrot'. Their height varies from 35 to 60 cm (14–24 inches) and they flower in mid to late spring. The shorter cultivars make good container plants.

DOUBLE LATE GROUP

Like the Double Early Group, these tulips have a bunch of petals clustered at the tip of the stem but they tend to be neater and more compact. They also flower later, in mid to late spring. The Double Late tulips are sometimes called peony-flowered tulips and their blooms do resemble the flowers of a double peony, more so than the early doubles. Stem heights vary but the late doubles are usually taller than the early doubles, although there is some overlap with a tulip like 'Red Princess' having a stem of around 35 cm (14 inches). Other late doubles have stems 50 or 60 cm (20–24 inches) tall and the flowers look good in cloudy weather as well as in the sun. In bedding, they make good companions to Single Late and Parrot tulips and the shorter cultivars make great container plants.

Double Late tulip 'Chatto'

Double Late tulip 'Orange Princess'

Kaufmanniana tulip 'Giuseppe Verdi'

Kaufmanniana tulip 'Showwinner'

KAUFMANNIANA GROUP

Tulipa kaufmanniana was introduced into cultivation in the late nineteenth century and, along with another introduction, *T. greigii*, it was soon used to breed a range of new cultivars. Those that show characteristics of *T. kaufmanniana* are placed in this group. They are among the earliest tulips to flower and have a short stem, typically 20 to 25 cm (8–10 inches) tall. The funnel-shaped flower is composed of long, upright petals that often have a red or purple flush on the back of the outer three. Inside there may be a yellow blotch, sometimes with further red markings. *Tulipa kaufmanniana* is known as the waterlily tulip and when the flowers open up the petals spread out to form a star. Some forms have bright red flowers, like 'Showwinner', while others have yellow or white flowers with red markings inside and on the back of the outer petals. The lance-shaped leaves may be plain green or blue-green but they often have dashes and streaks of purple, showing the influence of *T. greigii* in their breeding. It is the flower shape and flowering time that place these tulips in the Kaufmanniana Group.

Fosteriana tulip 'Sweetheart'

Fosteriana tulips 'Flaming Purissima' and 'Madame Lefeber'

FOSTERIANA GROUP

Tulipa fosteriana was introduced from Central Asia at the beginning of the twenti-eth century and naturally has a large, glossy red flower that was immediately put to good use to create new large-flowered cultivars, such as the Darwin Hybrids. Tulips in the Fosteriana Group are similar to the species but come in a range of colours, from the bright red of the original, like 'Madame Lefeber', to orange, yellow, white, and bi-coloured blooms, such as 'Sweetheart' and the wonderful 'Flaming Purissima'. The stems are typically between 45 and 55 cm (18–22 inches) tall and hold the flower above the broad leaves. They flower in mid-spring and generally last well in the garden with-out the need to lift the bulbs in summer. This makes them well suited to a mixed border, as well as an impressive bedding display.

Greigii tulip 'Fire of Love', with variegated and mottled leaves.

Greigii tulip 'Cape Cod'

Tulipa orphanidea, a species from southeast Europe and Turkey

GREIGII GROUP

The cultivars in this group resemble *Tulipa greigii*. Characteristics of this species include the flower forming a double bowl, with the inner three petals held more upright than the outer three, which arch back as the flower opens. The petals are wider and less pointed than in the Kaufmanniana tulips and they flower in mid-spring on a short stem, typically around 30 cm (12 inches) tall. The leaves are mottled with dashes and streaks of purple. This is a popular group of tulips and they come in many colours, from the simple red bloom of 'Red Riding Hood' to bi-coloured flowers like 'Cape Cod' and 'Quebec'.

MISCELLANEOUS GROUP

This group contains all the species tulips and the hybrids between them that don't fit with any of the other groups, such as 'Little Beauty' and 'Little Princess'. The species vary hugely in flower shape and size, flowering time, and cultivation requirements. The first tulips to flower are in this group, in particular *Tulipa biflora* and its close relatives, which have starry white flowers with a yellow centre and can bloom in late winter. The last tulip to flower is also in this group, *T. sprengeri*, which opens in early summer. In between these is the whole range of wild tulips, some of which make good garden plants if the right conditions can be found, while others may need to be grown in a cool glasshouse or cold frame to keep the bulbs dry when they are dormant. Most do not have the impact of the dazzling tulip cultivars and you wouldn't use them in bedding but the species have a charm of their own that is best appreciated close up, in a raised bed, rock garden, or pot.

Tulip Groups by Season of Bloom

EARLY SPRING
  Double Early Group
  Kaufmanniana Group
  Single Early Group
  Tulipa biflora
  Tulipa turkestanica

  Parrot Group
  Triumph Group
  Tulipa acuminata
  Tulipa clusiana
  Tulipa linifolia
  Viridiflora Group

MID-SPRING
  Darwin Hybrid Group
  Fringed Group
  Greigii Group
  Fosteriana Group
  Lily-flowered Group

LATE SPRING
  Double Late Group
  Single Late Group
  Tulipa sprengeri
  Tulipa tarda

Tulipa saxatilis 'Lilac Wonder', a selection of the best pink tulip species, with white-flowered *Narcissus* 'Toto'

100 TULIPS
FOR THE
GARDEN

For pure impact in spring, the tulip is the plant to grow. It comes in almost every colour, the exception being true blue, although some forms come very close. Plant tulips in a single colour block for a bold display or arrange them in geometric shapes of contrasting primary colours to jolt the senses.

The tulip can be subtle too. Delicate shades of varying hues can combine for a dreamy effect, or mix tulips with other spring-flowering bulbs and perennials to lift a border from its winter slumber. Whether in formal bedding, a mixed border, or in containers, the tulip provides all the colour you need, but it is when tulips are planted with surrounding plants taken into consideration that the overall effect is most memorable. Think of a colour scheme and there will be a tulip to make it happen.

The following 100 tulips have been chosen to show the variety not just in the shade of each colour but also in flower shape, size, and bloom time. These tulips may have flowers in one colour or the petals may be feathered and flamed with one colour over another. The plant descriptions are grouped according to which colour the overall effect comes closest: red, pink, purple, white, yellow, or orange.

The height given in the descriptions is the size of the tulip when it flowers, but height can vary depending on the amount of light available, the vigour of the bulb, and prevailing weather conditions.

The flowering season is also just a guide and it too can vary from year to year. For example, early tulips can be delayed by a cold spring and thus flower at the same time as mid-season tulips. In years when the weather warms up quickly after a long cold spell, a whole range of tulips can be seen flowering together, with the last of the early tulips still blooming as the first of the late-season tulips begin to open.

Tulips at the Keukenhof garden in Holland, showing just some of the colours found in these flowers.

Alternatives to the described and illustrated plants are listed with each description because the plants offered in shops and catalogues can change from year to year. A tulip may fall out of favour, stocks may become diseased, or a cultivar may simply be superseded by a newer, stronger one. Nevertheless, some tulips have been around for 100 years or more and show no sign of losing popularity; you can't go wrong with these but it's always worth looking out for any new tulips that the breeders have created. Unless otherwise stated, alternative plants belong to the same group as the described plant.

In the United Kingdom, the Royal Horticultural Society (RHS) gives the Award of Garden Merit (AGM) to plants considered especially garden worthy and this is noted in the descriptions if applicable but don't restrict your choice to those with this award. With tulips, the large range available means there is plenty of choice to add real value to the garden.

RED

Red is the colour of fire, danger, and of course love. Who doesn't love a red tulip? Red can mean scarlet or crimson but it can also be dark and moody, with hints of purple, or bright and sunny, verging on orange. The whole range is included in the tulips here. Pure red is a very intense colour and needs to be used carefully in the garden, otherwise it can be overwhelming. The foliage of tulips can offset the intensity of the red flowers so plant the bulbs to allow the leaves to be seen through the blooms.

Tulipa 'Showwinner'

A striking, cardinal red to scarlet flower, with a buttercup yellow base, held on a short stem above mottled leaves makes 'Showwinner' a real showstopper in early spring. Tulips in the Kaufmanniana Group are among the first to bloom, and the bright red flowers of this cultivar provide a vibrant start to the tulip season. It was registered in 1966 and has the AGM. The pointed petals are upright until the sun hits them and they open up wide to form that waterlily shape typical of *Tulipa kaufmanniana*. Red is an imposing colour so this tulip needs careful placing, flowering at a time of year when more subtle shades are the norm.

GROUP Kaufmanniana

HEIGHT 25 cm (10 inches)

BLOOM TIME Early spring

CULTIVATION To make the most of any early spring sunshine and entice those glorious blooms to open wide and reveal their yellow centre, plant this tulip in a sunny position but protect it from strong winds if possible. Good drainage and fertile soil should ensure it comes back in following years if planted out permanently.

LANDSCAPE AND DESIGN USES The bright flowers can be a little jarring outside of a bedding scheme, but luckily this is the perfect tulip for growing in containers. The short stature and relatively large flowers make a great display in pots on a patio or terrace. This tulip goes well with large Dutch crocus or white anemones, which can be planted in the same container. Once the tulip's flowers are over, you can simply move the pot out of the way and replace it with a display of a later-flowering variety.

ALTERNATIVES 'Scarlet Baby' has pinkish red flowers and 'Love Song' has more orange-red blooms.

Tulipa 'Ali Baba'

Such a bright, eye-catching splash of pure red can be provided by a number of tulips, but 'Ali Baba' has an attractive combination of a large flower held on a short stem above blue-green leaves streaked and dotted with purple dashes. This is one of the earlier Greigii hybrids, registered in 1955, and it has the AGM. The flower is the typical shape of tulips in the Greigii Group, with distinct inner and outer petals. On their outer surface, the petals are rose-red but on the inside, they are scarlet, giving way to yellow at the base with a small dark blotch.

GROUP Greigii
HEIGHT 30 cm (12 inches)
BLOOM TIME Early to mid-spring
CULTIVATION Grow in fertile, well-drained garden soil. When kept reasonably dry in summer, the bulb can persist for several years without lifting.
LANDSCAPE AND DESIGN USES This tulip can be grown among herbaceous perennials in a sunny mixed border. It makes a good bedding plant, especially where a shorter variety is desired, such as in a low-level planting around the base of a deciduous tree, mingled with other spring bulbs that flower at the same time. It looks particularly effective planted with pale blue *Muscari* or white *Anemone blanda*. It is also good for a container. For a more permanent display, try it in a mixed border, where it will flower alongside spring perennials like *Pulmonaria*, *Epimedium*, and the first blooms of *Dicentra formosa*.
ALTERNATIVES 'Red Riding Hood' is a popular, carmine red-flowered tulip and 'Toronto' has a coral pink flower. Both also have the AGM. 'Fire of Love' has a bright red flower held above startlingly variegated leaves displaying purple dots and dashes on a blue-green background with yellow margins.

Tulipa 'Madame Lefeber'

SYNONYM *Tulipa* 'Red Emperor'

'Madame Lefeber' is a fine early selection of *Tulipa fosteriana*, a magnificent red tulip from the hills around Samarkand in Uzbekistan. The large, shiny red flower has a dark blotch margined with yellow in the centre and is held on a tall stem above wide, grey-green leaves. In fact, the leaves are among the widest in the genus, but they don't detract from the plant, as the flowers are equally impressive. This tulip has been firmly established in cultivation for over 100 years, since 1905.

GROUP Fosteriana
HEIGHT 55 cm (22 inches)
BLOOM TIME Mid-spring
CULTIVATION Good drainage and full sun are best but this tulip is well adapted to a range of conditions, as long as damp, heavy soil and shade are avoided. When planted in the right place it will keep coming back.
LANDSCAPE AND DESIGN USES Aside from bedding displays, this tulip can be grown in a variety of locations. Scatter it along the foot of a sunny wall or through long grass under deciduous trees. In a mixed border or gravel garden, the bright red flowers stand out in mid-spring, combining well with silvery foliage of other sun-loving and drought-tolerant plants.
ALTERNATIVES 'Soroptimist' is a bright, tomato red tulip.

Tulipa 'Apeldoorn'

The single, bowl-shaped flower is typical of the Darwin Hybrid Group—gloriously big, brightly coloured, and held on a strong stem in mid-spring. It may have been around for well over half a century, but this old favourite still warrants a space in your border. The cultivar was raised by D. W. Lefeber and Company, and the name registered in 1951. It has given rise to a long list of sports with names like 'Golden Apeldoorn', 'Apeldoorn's Elite', and 'Beauty of Apeldoorn' but the original, cherry red form is still one of the most popular tulips. Inside the flower, black anthers surround a large dark blotch, edged with yellow. It is what I imagine when I think of a typical tulip and it really has earned its place in the garden.

GROUP Darwin Hybrid
HEIGHT 55 cm (22 inches)
BLOOM TIME Mid-spring
CULTIVATION Normal border conditions suit this tulip, whether in bedding or a mixed border. Being a Darwin Hybrid it can persist in the garden longer than some other tulips, so choose a spot that has plenty of sun and is never waterlogged.
LANDSCAPE AND DESIGN USES 'Apeldoorn' is a good bedding tulip. The single colour lends itself to numerous combinations so mix it with yellow or white daffodils or tulips in a range of different shades. When the bedding has finished, dig up the bulbs and move them to a border, where you can scatter them through mixed plantings to give a splash of red in subsequent years.
ALTERNATIVES 'Parade' is another old red hydrid, as is 'Oxford', which has bright red flowers flushed with purple. Newer red tulips in this group include 'Lalibela' and the magnificent 'Red Impression'.

Tulipa 'Red Impression'

As the name suggests, this tulip really does make a lasting impression. With its huge, glossy red flower it looks like a bigger, bolder, and flouncier version of 'Madame Lefeber' or *Tulipa fosteriana* and surely that species has had a major influence in the breeding of this tulip. It is taller than the Fosteriana tulips and the inside of the flower is mostly uniform blood red, with a small dark blotch at the centre and almost black anthers. If you want a big, pure red tulip, then this is probably the biggest and reddest of them all. Registered in 1994, it is a sport of 'Pink Impression' and it has the AGM.

GROUP Darwin Hybrid
HEIGHT 55 cm (22 inches)
BLOOM TIME Mid-spring
CULTIVATION Grown as bedding, it can be planted in any good garden soil and a sunny position.
LANDSCAPE AND DESIGN USES The bold, flamboyant flowers ensure this tulip is primarily used as a bedding plant. If the influence of *Tulipa fosteriana* extends to this cultivar's adaptability in the garden, then it should do well in a mixed border, at the foot of a sunny wall, or around deciduous trees. Trying to integrate it with other perennials could be a challenge, as the flowers can be overpowering and, to be honest, look a little unnatural in a more informal setting.
ALTERNATIVES Other big red tulips in the group include 'Parade', 'Lalibela', and of course, 'Apeldoorn'.

Tulipa 'World's Favourite'

This wonderful tulip has a deep bowl-shaped bloom in radiant tomato red that has the finest, most delicate highlights of golden yellow along the petal margins. Inside at the base of the flower is a dusky olive green blotch, edged with yellow on the inner three petals, surrounding dark purple-black anthers. This may not yet be the world's favourite tulip but it should be. It was named in 1992, has the AGM, and is frequently exhibited at tulip shows, often winning an award. When I talk about a refined tulip flower, this is what I mean. There are many tulips with yellow-edged petals but few display such sophistication and restraint as this supreme cultivar. It glows on the show bench and in the garden, especially when highlighted by slanting shards of sunlight.

GROUP Darwin Hybrid
HEIGHT 45 cm (18 inches)
BLOOM TIME Mid-spring
CULTIVATION Plant in a sunny position in deep, well-drained soil. The large flower brings rich colour and vibrancy to any design but new bulbs need to be planted every year to maintain the impact. Left in the ground they will continue to flower for a few years, like many Darwin Hybrids, but the blooms usually diminish in size after their first year.
LANDSCAPE AND DESIGN USES This is a good bedding tulip and can be grown in a mixed border. The stem is at the shorter end of the range for a Darwin Hybrid, making it also a good choice for a large container, where the blooms can be appreciated close up. Place the pot where the sun can enhance the warm glow this flower provides.
ALTERNATIVES 'Ad Rem' has a similar colour flower but with a pinkish sheen on the outer surface of the scarlet petals, a black base inside, and yellow anthers, on stems that reach 60 cm (24 inches) tall.

Tulipa 'Couleur Cardinal'

This old favourite has a luscious red, cup-shaped flower, with pointed petals that are flushed with a gorgeous plum purple on their outer surface. It dates from as long ago as the mid-nineteenth century, and the fact it has remained in cultivation for so long is testament to its unfailing beauty and reliability in the garden. It is a compact plant with the stem holding the flower just above the grey-green leaves. Planted in bedding or a border, the dusky blooms are enriched by the sun shining thought them on a bright spring morning.

GROUP Triumph
HEIGHT 35 cm (14 inches)
BLOOM TIME Mid-spring
CULTIVATION Grow in fertile, freely draining soil in full sun.
LANDSCAPE AND DESIGN USES A good bedding plant, it is also appropriate for a border or gravel garden, where it may continue to flower year after year. It is well suited for both formal and informal designs, bringing a touch of luxury to the garden in spring. The deep plum red blooms mingle well with silver foliage plants and pastel shades of other spring flowers. The compact form makes it perfect for containers and it stands up well to unpredictable spring weather. Combine it with deep purple tulips, like 'Havran' or 'National Velvet', for a richly coloured display.
ALTERNATIVES Other red Triumph tulips include the taller 'Ile de France', the cardinal red 'Oscar', and 'Red Power', which has a purple bloom at the base of the flower.

Tulipa 'Ile de France'

Taller and a little paler than 'Couleur Cardinal' but no less beautiful, this tulip has a rich, wine red flower that is blood red on the inside. A purple tint, verging on deep pink, is more concentrated on the outer three petals, leaving the inner three mostly red with a hint of purple towards their edges. This gives the flower a two-tone effect, which is enhanced by the sun. Inside the flower, the pale creamy green ovary is surrounded by deep purple-black anthers. A strong, upstanding plant dating from 1968, 'Ile de France' makes a captivating display when massed together in a large group.

GROUP Triumph
HEIGHT 50 cm (20 inches)
BLOOM TIME Mid-spring
CULTIVATION Plant this tulip in full sun and well-drained soil. A position that provides some shelter from the wind will help to keep the flowers, on their relatively tall stems, looking good for longer.
LANDSCAPE AND DESIGN USES It is best as a bedding plant, where the effect of the blooms massed together creates a wonderful sight. Try it in a border, where a little more height is required in mid-spring.
ALTERNATIVES 'Cassini' is another good bedding plant with deep red flowers.

Tulipa 'Aladdin'

Among the elegant Lily-flowered tulips, 'Aladdin' stands out with its red petals edged with creamy white, which highlights the graceful shape of the curvaceous, vase-shaped bloom. The main colour of the petals is scarlet to pinkish red, with the outer three having a stronger pink tint than the inner three. The tall stems hold the blooms well above the ground. There are many other Lily-flowered tulips with pale margins on the petals but in 'Aladdin' the whitish margin is narrow, as if picked out with a delicate brush to emphasis the beauty of the flower. This tulip has been around for over 70 years.

GROUP Lily-flowered
HEIGHT 55 cm (22 inches)
BLOOM TIME Mid to late spring
CULTIVATION Plant in full sun and fertile, free-draining soil.
LANDSCAPE AND DESIGN USES Like all the Lily-flowered tulips, 'Aladdin' adds variety to a display of bedding, with the flowers of pointed reflexed petals contrasting with more cup-shaped or bowl-like blooms of the Darwin Hybrids and Single Late tulips. 'Aladdin' looks particularly effective in a container, which is how I have grown it, and it gives a feel of the orient when planted in large rounded urns and set on a terrace or patio.
ALTERNATIVES 'Aladdin' has given rise to the sport 'Aladdin's Record', which has blood red flowers edged with primrose yellow and makes a suitable alternative.

Tulipa 'Pieter de Leur'

This must be one of the shortest Lily-flowered tulips but the richly coloured flower is still a good size, with the elegant pointed petals you would expect from a tulip in this group. The petals are blood red with a hint of reddish purple towards the tips, especially on the outer three. Inside the flower is an ivory white centre stained with a smudge of bluish grey. The anthers are dark purple-blue. The size makes this tulip special. It has the stature of a Kaufmanniana tulip but blooms mid to late season and with a flower typical of taller Lily-flowered cultivars.

GROUP Lily-flowered
HEIGHT 25 cm (10 inches)
BLOOM TIME Mid-spring
CULTIVATION It will survive without lifting in summer, as long as the soil is well drained.
LANDSCAPE AND DESIGN USES The perfect size for a container, this tulip has a sturdy stem and large flower that makes a colourful show on a patio or terrace. In an informal border it can flower with spring perennials and other mid-spring bulbs like *Muscari* and late daffodils. It is less easy to incorporate in bedding because most tulips that flower at the same time are taller, but on its own it can make an attractive display.
ALTERNATIVES Other Lily-flowered tulips with red flowers, like 'Red Shine' and 'Mariette', tend to be taller than 'Pieter de Leur'.

Tulipa 'Red Shine'

If you combine the luxurious, velvety red of 'Couleur Cardinal' and 'Ile de France' with the flower shape and taller stems of the Lily-flowered tulips, you get the lovely 'Red Shine'. Deservedly popular, it has been around for over 60 years and is widely available. The colour is a deep ruby red with a satin sheen, almost purple in certain light but with the name 'Red Shine', I couldn't really put it in the purple category. The pointed petals are not as long and spidery as they are in some Lily-flowered tulips but when fully open up in the sunshine, the flower has the characteristic vase shape with a narrow waist before the petals arch outwards.

GROUP Lily-flowered

HEIGHT 55 cm (22 inches)

BLOOM TIME Mid to late spring

CULTIVATION The usual requirements of sun and good drainage apply to this tulip. Some Lily-flowered tulips do come back and flower for several years in a border if the conditions are right and the soil is fertile and not too wet in summer.

LANDSCAPE AND DESIGN USES Mix 'Red Shine' with white or pink tulips, such as 'White Triumphator' or 'China Pink', which will flower at the same time. It looks good in formal bedding, a container, or the more relaxed planting of a mixed border.

ALTERNATIVES This cultivar is commonly offered for sale so there shouldn't be a problem finding it. Similar Lily-flowered tulips include 'Merlot', with more wine red flowers, and the deep ruby red 'Lasting Love'.

Tulipa 'Rococo'

A wonderful and intriguing tulip, the contorted flower is carmine red, flushed with velvety purple, especially at the centre of the outer three petals, and flecked with splashes of yellow and green along its crumpled edges. This is a fascinating tulip to look at, and I think one of the best in the Parrot Group. The flower is large and well rounded when it starts to open but in the warmth of the sun the outer petals can reach right out to display their bizarre shape fully. Every one is slightly different, with variation in the patterning and form of each bloom. The short stem and the dusky purple and red colour of the flower come from 'Couleur Cardinal', from which this is a sport, named in 1942.

GROUP Parrot
HEIGHT 35 cm (14 inches)
BLOOM TIME Mid-spring
CULTIVATION Plant in full sun or light dappled shade, and fertile, free-draining soil.
LANDSCAPE AND DESIGN USES The compact stature makes this tulip perfect for growing in containers. Pack as many as you can into a large pot for the best effect and use new bulbs every year. In bedding, the variable flowers make it more suited to an informal scheme so combine it with dark, leafy wallflowers or scatter it through a border of mixed early-flowering perennials. Garden expert Anna Pavord suggests planting it in front of a copper beech hedge or with the bronzy leaves of *Carex buchananii*.
ALTERNATIVES This cultivar is widely available, but there are other tulips with similar colouring, such as 'Doorman's Record' and 'Glasnost', although you may struggle to find them for sale.

Tulipa 'Red Spring Green' ▾

When I first saw this tulip, I was struck by the blend of rich pinkish red with a broad flash of pale green spreading from the base of the flower and a darker band up the centre of each outer petal. Inside the flower, the creamy white stigma contrasts with the dark purple anthers. On paper this blend of colours may sound less than harmonious but, as is often the case in tulips, the reality is actually quite pleasing and certainly distinctive. The flower isn't particularly large but planted in a group this tulip can still make an impact and makes an attractive combination with its stable mate 'Yellow Spring Green'.

GROUP Viridiflora

HEIGHT 50 cm (20 inches)

BLOOM TIME Late spring

CULTIVATION This tulip requires fertile, well-drained soil and full sun. To ensure a dry summer rest, it is best to lift the bulbs once the leaves have died down and store them somewhere cool and dry until autumn.

LANDSCAPE AND DESIGN USES Plant 'Red Spring Green' in a large container, a border, or a bedding display, either on its own or with other Viridiflora tulips that flower at the same time. Try it with a Single Late cultivar like the dark purple 'Queen of Night' to create a luxurious combination of strong, dark colours.

ALTERNATIVES 'Esperanto' is a possible substitute but has deeper red flowers and much darker green flames spreading from the base. The petals are longer and more pointed and the leaves have a thin white margin.

Tulipa 'Red Princess' ◄

This double tulip has a full, rounded flower of rich blood red, tinted with cardinal red on the outside. The flower is densely packed with petals and, being all one colour with no contrasting flames or petal margins, it is one of the more simple looking double tulips. That strong red bloom is held on a short stem, especially for a tulip that flowers in the second half of spring, making a compact plant perfectly suited to containers. Named in 1990, it is a sport of the double 'Orange Princess', which itself is a sport of the Triumph tulip 'Prinses Irene'.

GROUP Double Late
HEIGHT 35 cm (14 inches)
BLOOM TIME Mid to late spring
CULTIVATION The shorter stem, compared to many late flowering tulips, gives 'Red Princess' some resistance to the wind so it can be grown in a sunny open position. Plant in fertile, free-draining soil and lift the bulbs in summer to dry them off.
LANDSCAPE AND DESIGN USES This is a perfect container plant, compact and with a strong colour. Use it for a late-spring display around the outside of the house, on a patio, or in a porch, even in a window box. The full, double flowers have a presence even in dull weather so make a good display in formal bedding. In a mixed border they look less at home and probably won't last much more than a year or two anyway.
ALTERNATIVES There seem to be few red-flowered Double Late tulips regularly offered for sale, but the old 'Uncle Tom' and more modern 'Antraciet' come quite close, even if they are more purple than red and have taller stems.

Tulipa 'Red Georgette'

Multi-flowered tulips bring the bonus of up to six flowers from one bulb. They are not officially classed in their own group but in catalogues they are usually listed together. Most belong to the Single Late Group but there are some in other groups like Viridiflora and Triumph. 'Red Georgette' has up to four flowers of velvety cardinal red. The purple tinge is stronger on the outside of the young egg-shaped buds. As the flowers open they reveal their blood red insides and a greenish black blotch edged with yellow. Registered in 1983, this cultivar is a sport of another multi-flowered tulip, 'Georgette', which has yellow petals edged with red.

GROUP Single Late
HEIGHT 50 cm (20 inches)
BLOOM TIME Late spring
CULTIVATION The tall stem benefits from some shelter from strong winds.
LANDSCAPE AND DESIGN USES The flowers are smaller than those of most single-flowered tulips but they make up for it quantity. They look good in a container so plant up a large pot for displaying on a terrace or patio. The branching stem gives a slightly less formal look to bedding. The multiple blooms also make it a good cut flower.
ALTERNATIVES Another multi-flowered, Single Late Group tulip with red flowers is 'Wallflower'. The deep blood red 'Roulette' is in the Triumph Group and has slightly shorter stems.

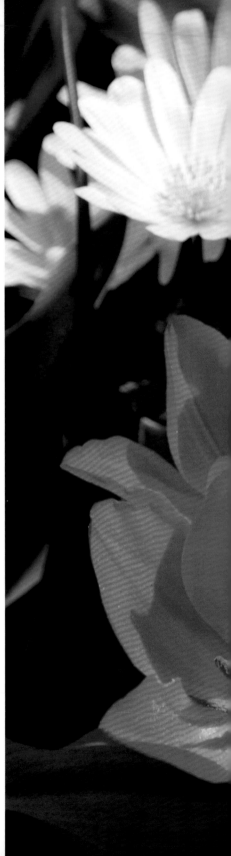

Tulipa linifolia ▲

The red form of this delightful species tulip has a bright, pure orange-red to scarlet flower that opens wide in the sun to form a shallow, gleaming bowl. The glossy petals have a pointed tip and at the centre of the flower is a small purple-black blotch. The short stem holds the flower above a cluster of long narrow leaves. This tulip comes from Central Asia and was first described in 1884. Its natural range extends from northern Iran, through Afghanistan, to the mountains of the Pamir Alai, but it has adapted well to cooler, wetter climates and is an AGM tulip.

GROUP Miscellaneous
HEIGHT 15 cm (6 inches)
BLOOM TIME Mid to late spring
CULTIVATION As long as the soil is well drained, this tulip will do well left in the ground. It needs a sunny position.
LANDSCAPE AND DESIGN USES The colourful flowers add a dramatic dash of red to a garden, but this is a short species so grow it near the front of a border or in raised planters, where it will not be overwhelmed by surrounding plants. It is ideal for a gravel garden. It can be also planted under deciduous shrubs or in the gritty soil of a raised bed or rock garden. In these situations it will continue to flower year after year.
ALTERNATIVES The named forms of *T. linifolia*, such as 'Red Hunter' (AGM) and 'Red Gem', are all very similar, varying slightly in the shade of red. Some catalogues list this species as *T. maximowiczii* but this is the same plant.

Tulipa praestans 'Fusilier'

Tulipa praestans is a popular and floriferous species producing a number of flowers from one bulb. Each flower is a clear, uniform orange-red, with no dark blotch at the centre, and 'Fusilier' has up to seven opening above the wide, mid-green leaves. The species was described in 1903 and originates from the mountains of the southern Pamir Alai in Central Asia. 'Fusilier' is a long-established and well-known form originally from Tajikistan. It is one of the most persistent in normal garden conditions and will keep blooming for many years, although the number of flowers per bulb may reduce over time. 'Fusilier' is an AGM tulip.

GROUP Miscellaneous
HEIGHT 30 cm (12 inches)
BLOOM TIME Mid-spring
CULTIVATION This tulip will survive in a range of conditions, from a hot, sunny border to dappled shade under deciduous trees or shrubs, or in grass. As long as heavy, poorly drained soil is avoided, it should survive from one year to the next.
LANDSCAPE AND DESIGN USES The bright flowers look best in a gravel garden or sunny mixed border, planted in random groups to create a naturalistic effect with other drought-tolerant plants. It will even do well at the edge of a woodland garden, as long as it is not in too much shade when in growth.
ALTERNATIVES *Tulipa praestans* 'Unicum' is a sport of 'Fusilier' with variegated foliage. Each leaf is edged with a thin white margin. Other forms of this species, like 'Van Tubergen's Variety' and 'Zwanenberg Variety', have slightly larger but fewer blooms.

Tulipa sprengeri

This enchanting species is the last to tulip to flower, holding on until
late spring or, in some years early summer, before opening its distinctive blooms, by which time most other tulips are have long finished. It
has a narrow funnel-shaped flower in the richest scarlet and the backs
of the outer petals are brushed with dusky beige. They open up in the
sun to reveal chunky yellow anthers. The flower is held above the narrow, glossy green leaves on an upright stem and, once the petals drop,
the fat seedpod develops, packed with flat seeds. This is one tulip that
does best with a little shade and some moisture in the soil, even in summer. First collected in the 1890s from northeastern Turkey and named
in 1894, *T. sprengeri* has not been seen in the wild since the early twentieth century. It is presumed extinct but survives in cultivation. It is
unique and irresistible.

GROUP Miscellaneous
HEIGHT 40 cm (16 inches)
BLOOM TIME Late spring to early summer
CULTIVATION The hot, sunny position and well-drained soil that most
tulips prefer are not the best conditions for *T. sprengeri*. This tulip does
best in light shade and fertile soil that retains some moisture year-
round. The bulbs resent disturbance and the most successful way to
introduce this plant is to scatter seed where you want it to flower.
LANDSCAPE AND DESIGN USES Grow it in dappled shade under deciduous trees and shrubs or among herbaceous perennials that will shade
the bulbs in summer. This is a tulip to combine informally with late-
spring perennials or it can be grown in grass where the bright blooms
will peer through the waving leaves.
ALTERNATIVES Not surprisingly, there are no real alternatives to this
tulip. Species like *T. orphanidea* have a similar habit but lack the purity
of colour and lateness of flowering that makes this such a unique plant.

PINK

Pink tulips can be a brash, dominating colour or a subtle hue that merges into a background of hazy spring flowers. Dark pink can almost be purple, while pale pink is almost white and within this group are white tulips that have streaks and speckles of pink spreading over the petals. It is bright, sugary pink that is the most commonly seen colour in these tulips and they make a wonderful combination with darker tones in a mixed display.

Tulipa 'Apricot Beauty'

Gorgeous, salmon pink blooms held on sturdy stems in early to mid-spring, make 'Apricot Beauty' a popular choice for containers and bedding. This tulip has been around for over 60 years and is still offered in most bulb catalogues as a strong and reliable, early season flower. It was named in 1953 and is a sport of the crimson pink 'Imperator'. Each bloom is a well-proportioned, rounded cup. The soft pink petals are delicately flushed with deeper, reddish pink, especially towards the centre, and fade to a pale lemon yellow at their base. It is an AGM tulip.

GROUP Single Early
HEIGHT 45 cm (18 inches)
BLOOM TIME Early to mid-spring
CULTIVATION Plant in full sun and fertile, well-drained soil but lift the bulbs for the summer.
LANDSCAPE AND DESIGN USES Fill a large pot with this tulip and place it on a terrace or by a doorway to bring some spring colour to the garden. It is also a great bedding plant but is unlikely to live long in a mixed border without lifting in summer once the leaves have died down. Store the bulbs somewhere cool and dry until autumn, or better still, buy new bulbs every year.
ALTERNATIVES 'Christmas Dream' is another good Single Early tulip but is shorter and has rose pink flowers. 'Candy Prince' has soft lilac flowers.

Tulipa 'Candy Prince'

Flowers of a wonderfully soft, luminous lilac purple make 'Candy Prince' a distinctive and desirable tulip. It blooms in the first half of spring on short stems, making it more resistant to the wind than many taller, later cultivars. The colour fades towards the edges of the petals and the base of the flower but there is not the strong contrast in colour seen in tulips like 'Christmas Dream', just that alluring pastel glow. The leaves are wide but well behaved. It is a relatively new cultivar, registered in 2001.

GROUP Single Early
HEIGHT 30 cm (12 inches)
BLOOM TIME Early to mid-spring
CULTIVATION Plant in full sun and fertile, free-draining soil. Lift the bulbs in summer to keep them dry or replant new bulbs every year.
LANDSCAPE AND DESIGN USES The short stems and distinctive colour make this tulip perfect for containers, put out on display when in bloom. In a border, plant it near the front so the flowers are not obscured by taller plants or create a low bedding display, mixing it with other bulbs, like later-flowering crocus, hyacinths, or anemones. Other Single Early tulips to combine with 'Candy Prince' include the deep, rich purple 'Purple Prince' or the pure white 'Calgary'.
ALTERNATIVES Other pink Single Early tulips like 'Christmas Dream' and 'Apricot Beauty' can be used as substitutes for 'Candy Prince' but they don't have the same wonderful soft lilac colour.

Tulipa 'Christmas Dream'

For a strong pink in a well-proportioned flower, look no further than this Single Early tulip. The large, egg-shaped bud opens to form a cup of rose pink flushed with fuchsia red and with a white base. The colour is most intense towards the centre of each petal but fades to paler pink at the margins to give the flower a distinctive two-tone effect. This long-lasting tulip is not especially tall so it can be planted in more exposed locations without risk of collapse. Named in 1973, it is a sport of the cherry pink 'Christmas Marvel'.

GROUP Single Early

HEIGHT 35 cm (14 inches)

BLOOM TIME Early to mid-spring

CULTIVATION Grow in a sunny spot and free-draining soil. Lift for the summer to keep the bulbs dry and replant the largest bulbs in autumn or buy new for a uniform display.

LANDSCAPE AND DESIGN USES The perfect bedding tulip, strong and reliable with long-lasting flowers held on a sturdy stem. It is also a good container plant for the same reasons. Mix with deep blue bedding plants for a strong spring colour scheme or combine it with deep purple tulips like 'Van der Neer' or 'Purple Prince'.

ALTERNATIVES Pink Single Early tulips include 'Candy Prince' and 'Apricot Beauty'. There are others but the range of tulips in this group offered in catalogues is limited compared to groups like Triumph and Single Late.

Tulipa 'Paul Rubens'

This is a tulip with pedigree. The old double 'Murillo' dates from 1860 and has given rise to a large number of sports in a range of colours, of which 'Paul Rubens' is one. Like other 'Murillo' sports, the flower is a loose, unruly collection of petals, like a handkerchief stuffed into the top pocket of a dandy's jacket. Each petal is deep pinkish red, fading to a wide creamy white margin. A dash of golden yellow can occasionally be glimpsed through the tussle of petals. This may not look much like a typical tulip but the wide bloom on a short, sturdy stem makes a colourful, long-lasting display.

GROUP Double Early
HEIGHT 25 cm (10 inches)
BLOOM TIME Early to mid-spring
CULTIVATION The short stem means this plant can withstand windy conditions. Plant new bulbs in free-draining soil each year to get the best show.
LANDSCAPE AND DESIGN USES Looking like a lavish summer flower but in a spring garden, the bloom of 'Paul Rubens' is a flamboyant addition to bedding, but plant it where it can get the most out of any early spring sunshine. Group it in a pot for displaying on a terrace or patio. Be wary of trying it in a more informal setting as those double blooms can look misplaced alongside more subtle spring flowers.
ALTERNATIVES There is a good range of Double Early tulips available and you can buy them as mixed colours but to get close to 'Paul Rubens' try 'Willemsoord', which is carmine red and white. It is a sport of cherry red 'Electra', which itself is a sport of 'Murillo'.

Tulipa 'Little Girl'

There are pale pinks, sugary pinks, and shocking pinks, and then there is the wonderfully restrained pastel pink of the gorgeous 'Little Girl'. This Greigii tulip is a recently named sport of the strong pink 'Sweet Lady'. It is short but with a large, wide flower of mid-pink with a hint of orange, over-laying a creamy white background. At the base of each petal is a small, brownish black blotch with a wide margin of delicate lemon yellow. As is typical of the Greigii Group, the inner three petals are more upright, forming a loose cup, with the outer petals slightly reflexed and more pointed. All this above wide leaves heavily marked with purple stripes. It is a subtle but enticing blend.

GROUP Greigii
HEIGHT 25 cm (10 inches)
BLOOM TIME Mid-spring
CULTIVATION To encourage those flowers to open wide and display their distinctive colouring, plant the bulbs in a sunny position. Fertile, free-draining soil is recommended if you want to keep this tulip going for more than one year.
LANDSCAPE AND DESIGN USES Plant it with other pink or white tulips to create a pastel combination or combine with purple tulips for more contrast. 'Little Girl is a short plant so be careful not to grow it with tulips that are too tall as companions. It looks great on its own or underplanted with white anemones or pale grape hyacinths (*Muscari*). It is also great for containers.
ALTERNATIVES It is hard to find an alternative pink Greigii tulip in a similar delicate shade. There are stronger pinks, such as the apricot rose 'Oratorio' or the claret rose 'Donau-perle', but they can't match the subtlety of 'Little Girl'.

Tulipa 'Flaming Purissima'

When I first saw 'Flaming Purissima' planted *en masse* in the Keuken-hof garden, I was struck by the great drifts of these huge flowers, some almost white and others a deep pink, like a billowing cloud of sugary candy floss. The flower starts out creamy white with just a faint hint of pink mottling towards the edges of the wide petals but as it ages the pink becomes stronger, creeping across the whole petal. The amount of pink is variable and in a large group of this tulip you will get a patchwork effect of pale and deeper pink blooms. The flowers are long lasting, just like those of another Fosteriana tulip, the white 'Purissima', from which this variation arose.

GROUP Fosteriana
HEIGHT 45 cm (18 inches)
BLOOM TIME Mid-spring
CULTIVATION This tulip has the resilience of the Fosteriana *Group* and is likely to reappear for several years if left in the ground. Full sun and fertile soil that drains well should provide the conditions for this tulip to thrive.
LANDSCAPE AND DESIGN USES It is really a plant for bedding, planted in wide drifts, with the large blooms crowded together to recreate that Keukenhof effect. If planted in a container, make it a large one and squeeze as many bulbs in the pot as possible.
ALTERNATIVES In the Fosteriana Group there is really nothing to compare to this tulip. The creamy white 'Purissima' is a wonderful tulip that has similarly large flowers but lacks the pink colouration.

Tulipa 'Russian Princess' ▲

This very special tulip is worth hunting down. The flower looks like it has been fashioned from the most delicate porcelain, softly painted with a flush of deep pink that gently fades to a translucent creamy white at the edges of each petal. Where the petals overlap, the colour looks stronger, with a heavier yellow tint along the margins. This flower adds a touch of refinement to a group that contains some of the most flamboyant and extravagant tulips and not surprisingly it has the AGM.

GROUP Darwin Hybrid
HEIGHT 50 cm (20 inches)
BLOOM TIME Mid-spring
CULTIVATION Planting in full sun and fertile, well-drained soil will help this tulip persist for a while in the garden. After flowering in bedding or a container, the bulbs can be transplanted to a sunny border.
LANDSCAPE AND DESIGN USES To really get close to its beguiling flowers this tulip needs to be grown in a container, placed on a sunny terrace, near a seat or doorway so you can appreciate the subtle colouring. Massed in a border or bedding scheme the effect of individual blooms can be diluted but it can be used as a contrast to the stronger colours of other spring bulbs.
ALTERNATIVES There is little in the Darwin Hybrid Group that comes close to this tulip except perhaps the pink and white 'Ollioules'. In the Triumph Group, 'Tropical Dream' has a similar, though less-refined, colour scheme.

Tulipa 'Shirley' ◄

Over pure ivory white, pinkish purple streaks and spots gradually spread from the edge of the petals, like ink soaking into blotting paper. This unique tulip is fascinating to observe as new blooms are mostly white, with only a thin line along the petal edge and a few small dots and dashes, but as the flower ages it becomes more suffused with purple. Inside the flower is a pale yellow stigma and dark purple-black anthers. Older flowers are heavily stained along their margin and with spots over the whole surface. Planted in a group, the overall effect is a pinkish haze but those individual blooms deserve your close attention. This tulip was first named in 1968 and is still popular today.

GROUP Triumph
HEIGHT 50 cm (20 inches)
BLOOM TIME Mid-spring
CULTIVATION Plant it in full sun and fertile, free-draining soil and it may live a few years in the garden, but new bulbs will create the best effect.
LANDSCAPE AND DESIGN USES 'Shirley' looks great on its own, planted in a parterre of low box hedging or around the base of a deciduous tree, peering through long grass. Combine with blue pulmonarias or the airy flower stems of Siberian bugloss (*Brunnera macrophylla*). Other Triumph tulips to mix with it include the rich purple 'Havran', lilac purple 'Passionale', or pristine 'White Dream'.
ALTERNATIVES It is hard to match the subtlety of 'Shirley' but 'Affaire' is a similar colour, though the staining is deep pink and more heavy-handed. 'Judith Leyster' is sugary pink over white but there are no dots and dashes, just a smooth stain spreading from the petal edges.

Tulipa 'New Design'

This large Triumph tulip has an impressive, wide, cup-shaped flower on a tall stem. It also has variegated foliage, with each leaf edged with a narrow white margin tinted faintly with pink. The overall flower colour is a strong pink but it is more complex than first appears, with deep pink washed over the pale yellow background that fades to pale pink towards the centre of each petal. Inside, the flower has a broad, creamy yellow base and a ring of dark brown anthers. This sport of 'Dutch Princess' was registered in 1974.

GROUP Triumph

HEIGHT 50 cm (20 inches)

BLOOM TIME Mid-spring

CULTIVATION This tulip requires full sun and well-drained soil. To maintain the effect created by the imposing blooms, replant every year with new bulbs.

LANDSCAPE AND DESIGN USES The large flowers stand out well in a mixed border or bedding scheme. Mix this tulip in a border of spring perennials like *Lathyrus vernus* and *Dicentra formosa*, and combine it with dark purple tulips, such as 'Negrita' and 'National Velvet' or the deep fuchsia pink 'Barcelona'.

ALTERNATIVES Pink Triumph tulips include the rose pink 'Innuendo' and the pale pink 'Rejoyce' but both are shorter plants. 'Barcelona' and 'Magic Lavender' are tall but have deeper, more uniformly coloured flowers. None of these have the variegated foliage but that's no great loss.

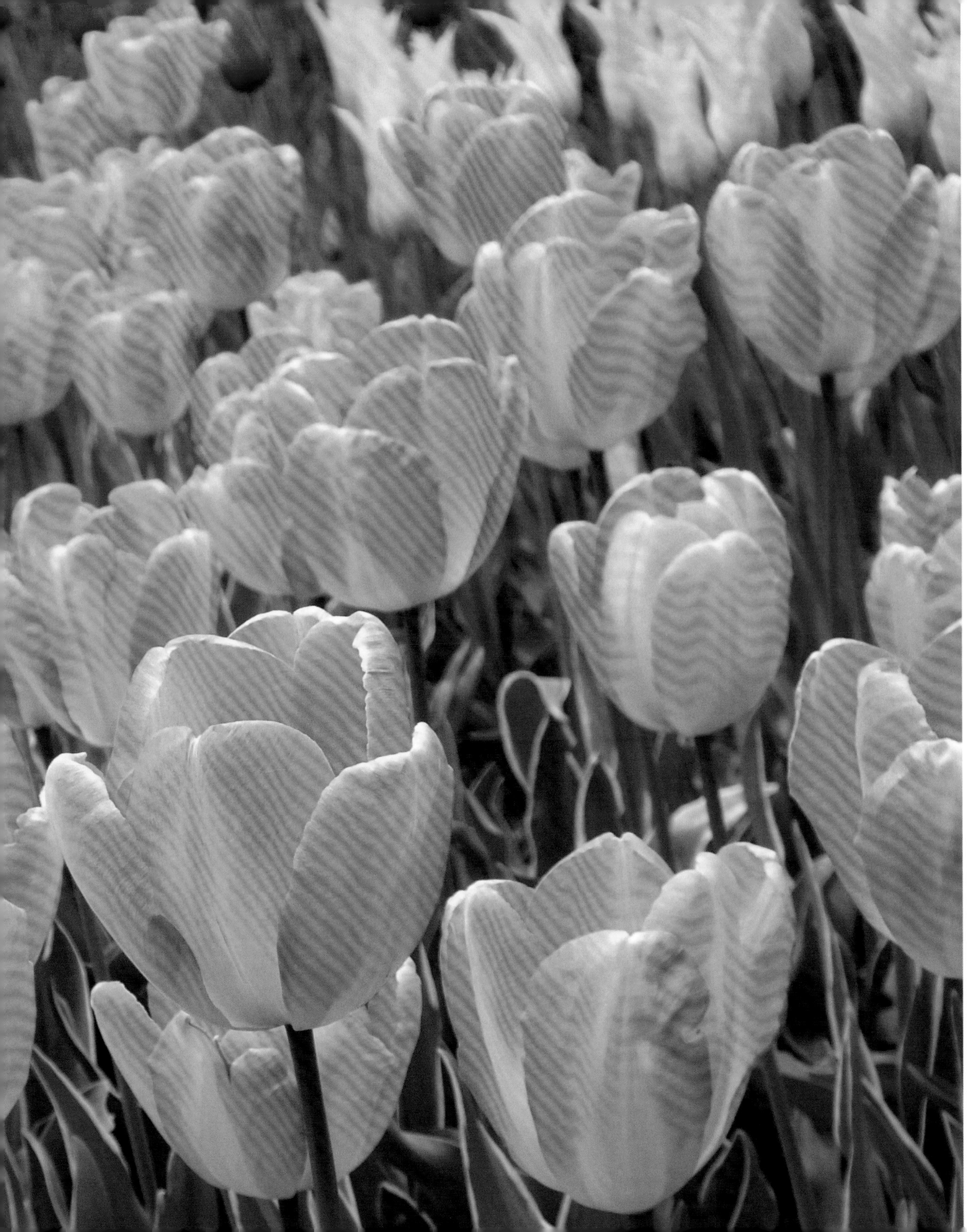

Tulipa 'China Pink'

Despite the many fancy new cultivars in the Lily-flowered Group, good old reliable 'China Pink' still remains one of the most popular and widely available. It was named in 1944, making it one of the older tulips in this group. The fluted blooms are a clear, rich rose pink, darkening slightly towards the middle of each petal. The flower is cup-shaped at first, but as it matures the pointed petals begin to arch outwards, held on sturdy stems above the upright, lance-shaped leaves. It makes a good cut flower and is an AGM tulip.

GROUP Lily-flowered

HEIGHT 45 cm (18 inches)

BLOOM TIME Mid to late spring

CULTIVATION The soil can range from gritty to deep and fertile, as long as it is not too wet and heavy. Give this bulb good light and drainage, and it can last for several years in a garden border.

LANDSCAPE AND DESIGN USES This tulip looks wonderful in formal bedding or in a large pot, the sturdy stems holding up well to adverse weather. Underplant it with purple violas or a deep blue like *Myosotis* 'Dwarf Indigo' and mix it with dark purple tulips like 'Purple Dream' or 'Burgundy'. It is suitable for a gravel garden or a mixed herbaceous border. Plant the bulbs so they grow through the young foliage of geraniums, epimediums, or white wood anemone (*Anemone nemorosa*).

ALTERNATIVES The Lily-flowered 'Yonina' has a reddish pink flower with pale margins to the long pointed petals or try 'Mariette', which is a deeper rose pink.

Tulipa 'Parrot Lady'

One of the more subdued Parrot tulips, 'Parrot Lady' has a flower of soft coral pink overlaying creamy yellow. The pink fades towards the crinkly margins of each petal and near the base gives way to golden yellow, especially inside the flower. This subtlety is welcome in the crazy parrots, which often have wild swirling colours broken up by the wrinkles and contortions of the petals. Like 'Rococo', it is one of the shorter Parrot tulips and makes a good cut flower.

GROUP Parrot

HEIGHT 40 cm (16 inches)

BLOOM TIME Mid-spring

CULTIVATION Grow in a sunny position in free-draining, open soil. Use new bulbs every year to guarantee flowering.

LANDSCAPE AND DESIGN USES A good tulip for a container, the relatively short stems hold up well in a breeze. In bedding it will benefit from being combined with a stronger colour, like the dark maroon-purple 'Black Parrot' or the bizarre 'Green Wave', which is a sport of the Viridiflora tulip 'Groenland' and has pink and white flowers with a wide green flame up each petal. For a more mooted scheme, try it with the white-and-green Viridiflora tulip 'Spring Green'.

ALTERNATIVES 'Silver Parrot' has predominantly white flowers edged with pink, the reverse of 'Parrot Lady'. 'Rai' has almost entirely rose pink flowers and is taller.

Tulipa 'Louvre'

This Fringed tulip has a flower of deep, rich purplish pink, fading slightly towards the frayed edges. The fringing is not as pronounced as in some other tulips in this group and the cut petals have a fine white margin. The base is white and the anthers a dark violet purple around the pale yellow stigma. This flower is not bright and glossy but deep and matt. The strong colour and the full cup-shaped bloom make this tulip stand out in bedding or a container. It is an AGM tulip.

GROUP Fringed
HEIGHT 45 cm (18 inches)
BLOOM TIME Late spring
CULTIVATION Plant the bulbs in full sun and well-drained, fertile soil.
LANDSCAPE AND DESIGN USES The Fringed tulips, with their bizarre frilly-edged petals, are not to my mind best used in a naturalistic planting design, such as growing through herbaceous perennials in a mixed border. However, they do look good in formal bedding and 'Louvre' is great in this situation, as well as in a container. Try it with a white tulip like 'Honeymoon' or a darker purple like 'Blue Heron' or 'Cuban Night'.
ALTERNATIVES Pink Fringed tulips include the popular 'Fancy Frills', which has a white central flame to each petal. 'Oviedo' is pale pink and white, flushed with lilac. 'Cummins' is pale purple rather than pink and the petals have a prominent white margin that is more deeply cut and spiky than in 'Louvre'.

Tulipa 'Drumline'

A compact head of overlapping petals form the shallow bowl-shaped bloom of this striking double tulip. Each petal is a wide lance shape of deep rose pink, deeper in colour along the centre and fading to a soft white margin. The colour scheme is not dissimilar to the Double Early tulip 'Paul Rubens', but the Double Late tulips are generally taller and the flower is more densely packed than the loose cluster of petals often seen in the early forms. 'Drumline' is a rounded head on a stick, especially before the flower has fully opened and surely a drumstick inspired the name. Planted in a large group, the effect is powerful, and being double, the flowers don't need the sun to open up. It is an AGM tulip.

GROUP Double Late
HEIGHT 40 cm (16 inches)
BLOOM TIME Late spring
CULTIVATION It can be planted in full sun or light, dappled shade and soil that is well drained, deep, and fertile.
LANDSCAPE AND DESIGN USES Plant 'Drumline' in a dense group, on its own, to create the best effect. The compact heads bumping together in the breeze form a swaying carpet of colour but can be damaged by strong winds. Underplant with purple or pink violas for a more traditional look, or use black-leaved *Ophiopogon planiscapus* 'Nigrescens' to set off those white-edged petals.
ALTERNATIVES There are many alternatives among the Double Late Group, including the paler 'Lady Fantasy', the rose pink 'Renown Unique', which has green flashes on the outer petals, and the soft pale pink 'Angelique'. 'Carnaval de Nice' is predominantly white but with flames of reddish purple up the centre of each petal.

Tulipa 'Menton'

The gorgeous 'Menton' is a superb, tall, late tulip. The colour is a smooth blend of pastel shades seamlessly merging into each other to create a flower of misty salmon pink with hints of pale orange along the petal edges. As the egg-shaped bud begins to open, the petals peel back like delicate parchment and eventually reveal the rose red interior and pale base of the flower. This is an AGM tulip, named in 1971 and still popular today. Like another great tulip, 'Avignon', it is a sport of the carmine red 'Renown' and has given rise to a sport of its own, 'Dordogne'. Together these make a noble family of Single Late tulips.

GROUP Single Late
HEIGHT 65 cm (26 inches)
BLOOM TIME Late spring
CULTIVATION Bulbs need to be lifted or replaced each year, as they will gradually fade away if left in the ground.
LANDSCAPE AND DESIGN USES The tall, stiff stem and simple flower make a fine late-spring display. Grow it with 'Avignon', 'Dordogne', and 'Renown' to create a luxurious combination of soft pink, claret red, pale orange, and rich purple. 'Menton' is best suited to bedding but also looks good in more informal planting.
ALTERNATIVES There is plenty of choice among the Single Late tulips and among the pinks are the strong coloured 'Pink Diamond', rose pink 'Survivor', and the wonderful 'Stunning Apricot'. Few are quite as tall as 'Menton' but they can be used to similar effect.

Tulipa aucheriana

With its small starry flower, this tiny species is the complete opposite to most garden tulips but it has a charm of its own and in the right place can make a captivating addition to the garden. The mauve pink to brownish pink flower is made up of pointed petals just 2 or 3 cm (1 inch) long and opens out flat in the sun. A cluster of bulbs will make an exquisite show of these diminutive blooms, held on short stems above the long, narrow, arching leaves. The species comes from Iran and first appeared in cultivation in 1880. It is closely related to *T. humilis* and is probably just a small version of that species, but the forms in cultivation are distinctive and it has received the AGM.

GROUP Miscellaneous
HEIGHT 10 cm (4 inches)
BLOOM TIME Mid-spring
CULTIVATION Like most tulips, this species needs sunlight and good drainage. The bulbs should be left in the ground to flower again the following spring.
LANDSCAPE AND DESIGN USES The small size means you have to be careful where you plant this species. It really does best given a dry summer so a raised bed or rock garden are both ideal. In these situations you can give it its own space where it isn't overshadowed by larger plants. Even better is growing it in a pot, using gritty soil and allowing it to dry out once the bulbs are dormant.
ALTERNATIVES The related *Tulipa humilis* comes in a range of colours, including mauve and violet pink, and the larger flowers make it more suited to growing in a border. Similar in size is *T. cretica*, with pale pink flowers held on short stems. It flowers a little earlier and benefits from some protection from the early spring weather.

Tulipa saxatilis 'Lilac Wonder'

Tulipa saxatilis is the best pink tulip species. The flower is a wide bowl of pointed candy pink petals that open flat in the sun to display a rich yellow central blotch edged with a thin white margin. The leaves are shiny green and appear above ground in early winter. The species is native to the Mediterranean island of Crete and southwestern Turkey, but a deeper pink form, called *T. bakeri*, is only found on Crete. 'Lilac Wonder' is a selection of the latter form but *T. bakeri* is now treated as a synonym of *T. saxatilis* and is sometimes listed as *T. saxatilis* Bakeri Group. I have been lucky enough to see both forms on Crete, growing in high-altitude meadows and clinging onto rocky ledges, but seeing it in the garden is the next best thing. 'Lilac Wonder' is an AGM tulip.

GROUP Miscellaneous
HEIGHT 20 cm (8 inches)
BLOOM TIME Mid-spring
CULTIVATION Dry, rocky habitats are this tulip's natural home and in the garden it does best in similar conditions so plant it in full sun and well-drained soil.
LANDSCAPE AND DESIGN USES It is perfect for a rock garden or raised bed but can be grown in a sunny border as long as it has a bright, open position, not crowded out by other plants. The bulbs seem to flower best if they are crowded together, so let clumps build up naturally without lifting.
ALTERNATIVES Apart from *T. saxatilis* itself, there is no real alternative to 'Lilac Wonder'. Some forms of *T. humilis* have pinkish or violet flowers with a yellow blotch but they are half the size or less.

PURPLE

This colour group includes some of the most desirable tulips, with irresistible deep, rich, velvety purple flowers. They can be the colour of ripe plums or suffused with dark maroon-red. This group also includes tulips described as blue, but make no mistake, although they have names like 'Blue Heron' or 'Blue Parrot', they are not blue but a light violet purple or mauve. So-called black tulips are also listed here but again, they are not true black but a very dark purple.

Tulipa 'Van der Neer'

A compact, egg-shaped flower of mid-purple, with just a hint of orange showing through near the tip of each petal, is held on a short sturdy stem, itself tinged with purple. The neat, pointed leaves are wavy edged and glaucous blue-green. All these attributes make it perfect as a short tulip for bedding, flowering in early to mid-spring. This old cultivar dates from 1860 but is still available and a reliable performer.

GROUP Single Early
HEIGHT 25 cm (22 inches)
BLOOM TIME Early to mid-spring
CULTIVATION This sturdy plant is able to withstand buffeting by the wind and rain that can occur in early spring. Grow in fertile, free-draining soil and an open, sunny position.
LANDSCAPE AND DESIGN USES The long-lasting flower and short stem make this tulip perfect for a container or early bedding. Individually the flower is not exactly spectacular but if you want a classic tulip to go in a traditional bedding scheme, then this is one to consider. The colour goes well with blue or white winter-flowering polyanthus or violas, or mix it with pink tulips like 'Christmas Dream' and 'Apricot Beauty' to lighten the mood.
ALTERNATIVES Among the Single Early tulips, 'Purple Prince' has beetroot purple flowers on slightly taller stems.

Tulipa 'Gavota'

A bold tulip with a reddish purple flame reaching up the centre of each petal, darker purple towards the base and giving way to a broad flash of rich sulphur yellow along the margins. The pointed buds open up to reveal their primrose yellow inner surface with a wide purple base and dark anthers. The neat blue-green leaves create a subtle backdrop to these striking, bi-coloured blooms. Named in 1995, this distinctive tulip has quickly become a popular choice and has the AGM.

GROUP Triumph
HEIGHT 45 cm (18 inches)
BLOOM TIME Mid-spring
CULTIVATION A sunny, well-drained border is best, but after its first year I have found it declines, especially if not in a very sunny spot. It may be better to lift and store the bulbs over the summer.
LANDSCAPE AND DESIGN USES Primarily a tulip for bedding or containers, it looks great against a brick wall or in a large terracotta pot. It is particularly effective on its own or you could plant it with other tulips that highlight the colours of 'Gavota', like the deep purple 'National Velvet' or the yellow, Lily-flowered 'West Point'.
ALTERNATIVES There is little else to recommend as an alternative to this unusual tulip except perhaps the Triumph tulip 'Reputation' that has red petals edged with yellow.

Tulipa 'National Velvet'

This is one of those purple tulips that verges on red, in this case a glowing, deep purplish maroon-red, lightly brushed with a lighter purple bloom on the outer surface of the petals to give that gorgeous velvety texture referred to in its name. The petals form a neat cup but in the warmth of the sun they slowly spread open to reveal their shiny maroon-red inner surface and the wide yellow blotch at the flower's centre that has a smudge of dark purple along its margin. The anthers are bluish purple and held on thick yellow filaments. A tulip of this rich colour is worth finding room for in any garden and it has the AGM.

GROUP Triumph

HEIGHT 40 cm (16 inches)

BLOOM TIME Mid-spring

CULTIVATION In all but the quickest-draining soils, it will benefit from being lifted for the summer, or plant it on a sunny bank or in a gravel garden to give it the best chance.

LANDSCAPE AND DESIGN USES Even if it only survives a few years, this tulip is worth trying in a mixed border just to have that wonderful colour in your garden. It is ideally suited to bedding or containers where it will have the greatest impact if you plant new bulbs every year, either on their own or combined with orange tulips, like 'Ballerina' or Prinses Irene'.

ALTERNATIVES In the Triumph Group 'Passionale' has neat, lilac purple flowers and 'Negrita' has deeper purple blooms the colour of beetroot.

Tulipa 'Flaming Flag'

From a green, egg-shaped bud, the flower develops into a pleasing combination of dark purple streaks and flames and lighter purple smudges over a pure white background. The purple is darkest at the centre of each petal where the flame reaches up from the base and is surrounded by a more delicate tint of mid-purple with dark flashes that reach out to the white margins. This new cultivar was registered in 2007 and is a sport of 'Purple Flag'.

GROUP Triumph
HEIGHT 45 cm (18 inches)
BLOOM TIME Mid-spring
CULTIVATION Give it plenty of sun and good drainage, and lift in summer to keep the bulbs dry.
LANDSCAPE AND DESIGN USES The neat rounded flowers look good in a container, on its own or mixed with other tulips, like the dark purple 'Negrita' or 'National Velvet'. It may survive a few years in a mixed border, but the purple-flamed flowers don't always mix well with other spring flowers. Try it with evergreen grasses like *Festuca glauca* or a bronzy-leaved sedge like *Carex comans* to make an appealing combination.
ALTERNATIVES The nearest alternative is 'Rem's Favourite', sometimes listed as 'Zurel'. It has a harsher colouring than 'Flaming Flag', with strong, dark purple flames over a white background but without the transition zone of lighter purple. 'Happy Generation' has more pinkish red flames over white.

Tulipa 'Havran'

A lovely deep plum purple tulip, a little like the Single Late 'Queen of Night' but flowering earlier and on the shorter stem typical of the Triumph tulips. The flower is a narrow cup and the pointed petals give it an elegant shape as it opens. The backs of the petals have a bluish purple bloom so the flower has a luxurious velvety appearance, and it can have two or three flowers per bulb. Inside the flower is a small yellow blotch and dark anthers. This relatively new cultivar was registered in 1998.

GROUP Triumph

HEIGHT 45 cm (18 inches)

BLOOM TIME Mid-spring

CULTIVATION I have never tried it in a mixed border, but it reportedly survives in the ground and keeps flowering for a few years at least. It will require the usual sunny position and fertile, free-draining soil to do well.

LANDSCAPE AND DESIGN USES This strongly coloured tulip can provide a backdrop for a range of dusky companions. For a truly rich scheme, pair it with the velvety red 'Couleur Cardinal' or the brownish orange 'Brown Sugar'. For a lighter mood, try it with 'Shirley' or 'Flaming Flag'. Grow it in a large container for dramatic effect.

ALTERNATIVES For deep purple Triumph tulips you can also try the even darker 'Ronaldo' or the maroon-black 'Paul Scherer', which has the AGM.

Tulipa 'Claudia'

With their purple flowers edged with white along the margins of the long, pointed petals, 'Claudia' and 'Ballade' are very similar looking Lily-flowered tulips. Of the two, 'Ballade' is the oldest, best known, has the AGM, and is more frequently offered, but 'Claudia' is becoming more widely available and may well supersede it. Only time will tell. 'Claudia' has a slightly darker violet purple flower with a hint of red. The petal margins have a wide, white border, highlighting the vase-like shape of the flower and inside is a yellow blotch at the base. This tall but sturdy tulip has a broad flower that can really make an impact.

GROUP Lily-flowered
HEIGHT 55 cm (22 inches)
BLOOM TIME Mid to late spring
CULTIVATION This tulip needs a sunny spot with reasonable drainage.
LANDSCAPE AND DESIGN USES If it is anything like 'Ballade', this tulip will settle down in a border and keep flowering for several years. Plant it so it grows through spring flowers like forget-me-knots (*Myosotis*) and pulmonarias. In bedding, mix it with other Lily-flowered tulips like 'Purple Dream' or 'White Triumphator', or plant it on its own. In a container it makes a mesmerizing show.
ALTERNATIVES If you can't find 'Claudia', you should find 'Ballade'. For more pink than purple flowers but still with a white margin, try 'Yonina'.

Tulipa 'Merlot'

Hold a glass of red wine, preferably a Merlot for accuracy, up to the sun, and the light shining through it will give the rich glowing colour seen in this tulip. The pointed petals form an elegant shape and are smooth carmine purple with a soft bloom of purple on their outer surface and a dark base inside. This new cultivar, named in 2008, is just starting to appear in catalogues. Like the Triumph tulip 'National Velvet', the flower is a wonderful, luxurious colour that deserves space in the garden. The petals are not drawn out into the long wispy points found in some tulips in the Lily-flowered Group, but they form a deep cup-shaped flower spreading outwards at the top. Now drink the wine.

GROUP Lily-flowered

HEIGHT 50 cm (20 inches)

BLOOM TIME Mid to late spring

CULTIVATION This tulip needs a sunny position but plant it where the low morning sun can shine through the bloom to give that wonderful glow. The bulb may persist for a few years if the soil is well drained.

LANDSCAPE AND DESIGN USES This tulip is good for bedding and containers but also worth a try in a mixed border. Combine it with a white tulip like 'White Triumphator' or the Fringed 'Honeymoon' for contrast. It goes very well with pink, such as 'China Pink' or the Triumph tulip 'New Design'.

ALTERNATIVES The Lily-flowered 'Purple Dream' has glossy violet purple flowers, with a white centre but it grows to a similar height. 'Pieter de Leur' is shorter than 'Merlot' and is really a red tulip but it has a hint of purple on the outer petals. 'Red Shine' has a little more purple in the flower and is an even better alternative.

Tulipa 'Burgundy'

This deep violet purple tulip has the perfect lily shape, with long narrow petal tips and a distinct narrow waist when the flower is closed. When the sun warms it up, the petals arch back, forming a wide star and exposing the pale yellow anthers and a creamy white base to the flower, edged with a dash of bluish purple. The leaves are also narrow and pointed, with a deep channel and often a wavy margin. 'Burgundy' is one of the darkest Lily-flowered tulips but although named as long ago as 1957, it isn't planted as often as you might think. You are more likely to see 'Purple Dream' or 'Maytime' but if you can get the right bulbs, 'Burgundy' is a lovely tulip to grow.

GROUP Lily-flowered
HEIGHT 50 cm (20 inches)
BLOOM TIME Mid to late spring
CULTIVATION In well-drained soil, this tulip tends to keep going if left in the ground.
LANDSCAPE AND DESIGN USES With its slim flowers, 'Burgundy' is not the showiest plant for bedding, which may explain its lack of popularity but it makes a fine container plant. Its persistence makes it suited to a mixed border, in a gravel garden or a raised bed, among silver foliage plants or the yellow and white spring blooms of primroses, anemones, and later-flowering daffodils.
ALTERNATIVES 'Maytime' is another dark purple, Lily-flowered tulip, but it is hard to find these days, having been replaced in many catalogues by 'Purple Dream', which is also a fine tulip but a little lighter in colour.

Tulipa 'Black Parrot'

A little mad, even by Parrot tulip standards, the crumpled flowers of 'Black Parrot' open up to a frilly plate of crazy twisted petals. It is not a large flower but this adds to its appeal, as you don't want to overdose on the gorgeously rich purple blooms. Their colour is a deep maroon-purple with spots of almost black inside the flower, hidden among the wrinkles along the mid-vein of each petal. The anthers are dark purple but the ovary is a creamy white and stands out at the centre of the tousled bloom. Named in 1937, it is a sport of the even older Single Late tulip 'Philippe de Comines' so is one of the later-flowering Parrot tulips. It has the AGM.

GROUP Parrot
HEIGHT 50 cm (20 inches)
BLOOM TIME Late spring
CULTIVATION The usual growing conditions of sun and fertile, free-draining soil are fine for this tulip but it is best lifted for the summer.
LANDSCAPE AND DESIGN USES Plant this tulip with blue or mauve flowers, in bedding or a container. Combine with a Single Late tulip like 'Menton' to add a lighter colour to the scheme. The rich maroon-purple goes with other colours, such as pink or yellow, so the possibilities are varied and you could try it with the Lily-flowered tulips 'China Pink' and yellow 'West Point'.
ALTERNATIVES There is little commonly available that can be substituted for 'Black Parrot'; the deep colour and wonderfully ruffled petals are just not found in other tulips. The closest are the lighter coloured 'Blue Parrot' and 'Muriel'.

Tulipa 'Blue Parrot'

This is one of those tulips that claims to be blue but is in fact purple, in this case a smooth bright violet purple to lavender mauve, with a distinctive faint bronze flush on the outside of the flower. It is a sport of the lilac mauve Single Late tulip 'Bleu Aimable' and was named in 1935. Appearing in late spring on tall stems, the petals are not as cut up as are those of some Parrot tulips, but they are twisted and contorted to form a broad, full flower. At the centre inside is a small patch of almost blue, but you can only see it when the flower is fully open. It is the unique colour that sets it apart and it remains a popular tulip.

GROUP Parrot

HEIGHT 55 cm (22 inches)

BLOOM TIME Late spring

CULTIVATION The tall stems may need some shelter from strong winds but otherwise, sun and well-drained soil are fine.

LANDSCAPE AND DESIGN USES Like most Parrot tulips it looks good in a container. Its height makes it a fine bedding plant too. Combine it with Single Late tulips like dark purple 'Queen of Night' or 'Renown' for a richly coloured late spring display. Underplant with dark blue violas and polyanthus or the bronzy purple foliage of heucheras.

ALTERNATIVES For a similar colour in the Parrot Group try the shorter 'Muriel', a sport of 'Blue Parrot' that has large, deep violet flowers tinged with purple-blue.

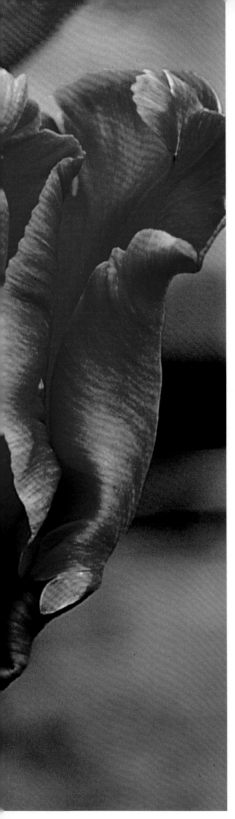

Tulipa 'Blue Heron'

Again, not blue but a shade of violet purple that fades towards the crystalline petal margins, which are pale lilac and finely cut, as is typical in the Fringed Group. The flower is two-tone but the transition is smooth and the main colour verges on blue in the same way as in 'Blue Parrot'. The flower forms a shallow cup, and in the sun the outer three petals arch back, leaving the inner three more upright. Inside, the base is white and the anthers black. This fine tulip dates from 1970 and has the AGM.

GROUP Fringed
HEIGHT 60 cm (24 inches)
BLOOM TIME Late spring
CULTIVATION Like most Fringed tulips, the bulbs do not survive long without lifting in summer.
LANDSCAPE AND DESIGN USES This tall tulip is ideal for bedding, providing an unusual colour that goes well with darker purples like 'Cuban Night' or the purple-and-white 'Cummins'. As previously stated, the Fringed tulips are not the best for a mixed border planting in my opinion. They make a novel container plant but the tall stems will need a tall pot to avoid looking out of scale.
ALTERNATIVES For a similar colour you need to go to the Parrot Group and 'Blue Parrot'. In the Fringed Group, 'Cummins' has pale purple flowers but with a prominent white frilly margin.

Tulipa 'Cuban Night'

This cultivar has the wonderful deep colour of 'Black Parrot' but in a Fringed tulip. The dark purple has a hint of maroon and there is a purple bloom on the outside of the petals. The flower forms a neat, shallow cup, with the crystalline margins of the petals in the same colour as the rest of the flower, all held above blue-green leaves. When the sun shines through them, the petals glow the colour of port. Dating from 2007, this new cultivar can be found in some catalogues but is surely going to become a popular choice once more people discover its magic.

GROUP Fringed
HEIGHT 55 cm (22 inches)
BLOOM TIME Late spring
CULTIVATION Lift the bulbs for the summer or better still, plant new bulbs in autumn for the best effect.
LANDSCAPE AND DESIGN USES It looks great on its own in a densely planted group or try combining it with other colours, like the deep pink 'Louvre' or the bright pink Lily-flowered 'China Pink'. In bedding or containers, plant the bulbs among blue grape hyacinths, anemones, or violas.
ALTERNATIVES More dark purple tulips are appearing all the time and among the Fringed Group are the bronze-purple 'Black Jewel' and the very new and very dark 'Vincent Van Gogh'.

Tulipa 'Uncle Tom'

From a tight spherical bud, the flower of 'Uncle Tom' opens out to form a colourful, wide bowl of overlapping petals. The Double Late tulips are sometimes called peony-flowered tulips and in this cultivar you can see why. The flower is filled with neatly arranged, rounded petals in an enticing maroon-red and the shape is just like a double peony. When the flower opens up, it reveals a bright yellow centre and violet purple anthers. This old tulip dates from 1939 and the flower is one of the more restrained doubles, not too frilly and with a large but not overweight bloom.

GROUP Double Late

HEIGHT 45 cm (18 inches)

BLOOM TIME Mid to late spring

CULTIVATION Plant in full sun but give it some shelter, as the relatively heavy flowers can be battered by the wind, causing the stems to bend down.

LANDSCAPE AND DESIGN USES Like all double tulips this is a great container or bedding plant. Mix it with 'Angelique', another Late Double tulip, for a lovely show of wine red and soft pink.

ALTERNATIVES 'Red Princess' could be used as an alternative, although it is a bright red. For a dark purple double, plant the tall 'Black Hero', a sport of 'Queen of Night' and a similar blackish hue.

Tulipa 'Queen of Night'

Named in 1944, this classic dark purple tulip is as popular now as it has ever been. The flowers may not be large but they are still among the darkest you will find and they have an elegant sophistication rarely matched by more modern cultivars. The stems are tall and hold egg-shaped buds that begin pale matt purple but soon develop their deep, rich aubergine purple colouring, with a dusting of dark purple bloom on the outside to give a texture of satin to the petals. The leaves are grey-green and make a great backdrop to a group of the neat, compact, dusky flowers. Don't be distracted by the new kids on the block; this old cultivar is tulip royalty and it still has a lot to give.

GROUP Single Late

HEIGHT 60 cm (24 inches)

BLOOM TIME Late spring

CULTIVATION The usual growing conditions for tulips are suitable for growing this timeless bulb but without lifting in summer, it will slowly dwindle in the garden.

LANDSCAPE AND DESIGN USES Plant this bulb anywhere you can grow tulips—in containers, bedding, or a sunny mixed border. I remember seeing it in a large pot with the Lily-flowered 'White Triumphator' and it looked particularly pleasing. The same combination would work in a bedding scheme, or try it with other dusky pinks and purples like 'Menton' and 'Renown'. It also looks good scattered randomly through a border, under deciduous shrubs or among spring flowers of *Dicentra* and yellow epimediums.

ALTERNATIVES Among the Single Late tulips are several dark purple cultivars, including 'Black Swan' and the slightly shorter 'Recreado'. The more recently named 'Cafe Noir' is almost black like 'Queen of Night'.

Tulipa 'Renown'

The wide petals of this boldly coloured, long-lasting tulip are carmine red with a hint of pinkish purple. The red colouration is strongest in the centre of the inner three petals, with the outer three having more of a pink hue, especially towards the margins. Inside at the centre of the flower is a dark purple-blue blotch and dark anthers surrounding a pale green ovary. The outer petals arch back in the sunshine, creating a double bowl effect reminiscent of the Greigii tulips. This cultivar was named in 1949 and has given rise to a number of sports, including 'Avignon', 'Menton', and the double 'Renown Unique', which are now more commonly grown than the original.

GROUP Single Late
HEIGHT 65 cm (26 inches)
BLOOM TIME Late spring
CULTIVATION Although sturdy, it is a tall tulip that will benefit from some shelter from strong winds. Plant it in a sunny, well-drained spot.
LANDSCAPE AND DESIGN USES This tulip is best used as a companion to its sports 'Avignon' and 'Menton' to add some depth to a pastel display in late-spring bedding or a large container. It can be planted on its own in a mixed border, around shrubs that will provide some protection.
ALTERNATIVES Although shorter and a darker purple, 'Recreado' could be used as an alternative from the Single Late Group.

Tulipa humilis 'Persian Pearl'

Tulipa humilis is a delightful species for the garden, with a wide starry flower on a short stem that comes in a range of colours from pale violet through mauve, lilac, magenta, and purple to deep red. The blotch inside the flower may be yellow or bluish black. Many of these variations have been named in cultivation and their small stature and colourful flowers gave them all a jewel-like quality. 'Persian Pearl' is one of the most popular, with deep magenta purple flowers and a bright yellow centre. The backs of the outer three petals are brushed with silvery grey. The species, which comes from Turkey, northeastern Iran, and south to Syria and Lebanon, was described in 1844. This cultivar was named in 1975.

GROUP Miscellaneous
HEIGHT 10 cm (4 inches)
BLOOM TIME Early to mid-spring
CULTIVATION A sunny position in the garden is important, but this tulip can be grown in soil that retains some moisture in the summer.
LANDSCAPE AND DESIGN USES It will need careful placing so as not to be lost among other plants but in the right position it can add a magical touch to the early spring garden. Plant it near the front of a border, in a gravel garden or on a raised bed, where the blooms can be easily seen. Different colour forms can be mixed to provide a colourful display, like a box of jewels. On its own in a pot 'Persian Pearl' is a stunner.
ALTERNATIVES The whole range of colour forms of *T. humilis* can all be used for the same effect and you won't be disappointed. 'Eastern Star' is a similar colour to 'Persian Pearl'.

Tulipa 'Little Beauty'

This lovely dwarf tulip has bright purple flowers that open up to reveal a distinctive bluish purple blotch in the centre of the flower, edged with a smudged white margin. In size and form it is close to *T. humilis*. The name was registered in 1991 by W. Van Lierop and Sons, who registered another small tulip in the same year, the orange-red 'Little Princess'. The latter is a hybrid between the variable species *T. orphanidea* and *T. aucheriana* (itself a form of *T. humilis*). 'Little Beauty' is probably the result of a similar cross, the natural colour variations in the two species giving rise to the two colour forms found in these cultivars. Whatever its origins, 'Little Beauty' is a charming tulip and it has the AGM.

GROUP Miscellaneous

HEIGHT 10 cm (4 inches)

BLOOM TIME Mid-spring

CULTIVATION Treat this little tulip in the same way as *T. humilis* by planting in full sun and free-draining but moisture-retentive soil.

LANDSCAPE AND DESIGN USES Find a spot where it isn't hidden by taller plants. Left in the ground to increase naturally it can form a delightful cluster of blooms in a gravel garden or raised bed and looks equally good in a pot. Mix it with 'Little Princess' for an orange and purple combination or plant it with different colour forms of *T. humilis*.

ALTERNATIVES The various forms of *T. humilis* can be used as an alternative to this tulip, especially those with a dark central blotch, like *T. humilis* Violacea Group black base. 'Little Princess' is a shade of orange rather than purple but otherwise very similar.

WHITE

From pure white to ivory and creamy yellow, these tulips brighten up any display by providing an uplifting highlight. Some have flashes of green or yellow on their petals and others may have a yellow blotch at the centre of the flower or red markings, but the overall effect is one of light and purity that can add glamour and sophistication to your garden.

Tulipa 'Ancilla'

The flower of 'Ancilla' is a pinkish white star with a bright yellow centre edged with a thin red line. The petals spread wide to form the typical waterlily shape of the Kaufmanniana tulips but when closed up the outer three petals show their reddish pink backs. The large flower is held on a short, sturdy stem, so it opens just above the broad, lance-shaped leaves. The blooms open early and this striking tulip makes a bright start to the tulip season. It was named in 1955 and has the AGM.

GROUP Kaufmanniana
HEIGHT 20 cm (8 inches)
BLOOM TIME Early spring
CULTIVATION Plant in full sun and fertile, well-drained soil.
LANDSCAPE AND DESIGN USES Use 'Ancilla' in an early spring bedding display, and when the sun shines, the flowers will open wide and white. In cloudy weather the flowers remain closed but they show off the rosy pink stripes on the backs of the petals, so you win either way. The short stem stands up to harsh weather and this tulip is perfect for a container or even a window box. It can also be grown in a raised bed or rock garden, where the bulbs can be left in the ground to flower for several years.
ALTERNATIVES Among the Kaufmanniana tulips 'The First' has white flowers with red-backed petals, and 'Concerto' has creamy white flowers.

Tulipa 'Verona'

This wonderful, fragrant, early double is usually described as yellow, but it is a very pale, soft yellow, more like ivory white. The flower is not neat and tidy but is formed of an irregular bunch of petals crowded together on top of a short stem. The petals have a satin-like quality, and look like they have been cut from the fine silk of a wedding dress. The petal margins undulate and are ivory white. The yellow colour becomes stronger towards their base and around the sulphur yellow anthers. Occasionally the outer petals have green markings. This cultivar was registered in 1991.

GROUP Double Early
HEIGHT 40 cm (16 inches)
BLOOM TIME Mid-spring
CULTIVATION This is one of the taller Double Early tulips so provide some shelter from the wind.
LANDSCAPE AND DESIGN USES Packed tightly in a container or as part of a bedding scheme, this tulip makes a display of soft, rounded blooms that merge with each other to create a silky white, fragrant cloud. Place a pot near a door or window so you can catch the scent as the blooms are warmed by the sun. If you want a mixed group of Double Early tulips, choose plants that reach a similar height, such as the rosy pink 'Foxtrot' or the slightly deeper yellow 'Montreux'.
ALTERNATIVES 'Montreux' has more yellow in the flower but it is still a subtle and intriguing double tulip. For pure white, you could use 'Mount Tacoma' or the shorter 'Cardinal Mindszenty'.

Tulipa 'Purissima'

SYNONYM *Tulipa* 'White Emperor'

'Purissima' is one of the most impressive white tulips, with a huge, sumptuous, creamy white bowl held on a sturdy stem. Up the centre of each petal is a lance-shaped band of pale yellow that is especially prominent on the outer three. The yellow is strongest on young blooms and tints the whole petal, but as the petals age, the colour fades to leave a mostly white flower. Inside, the yellow deepens towards the base, around the long, thin, black anthers. With the sun shining through them, the flowers of this tulip are dazzling, creating a shimmering white carpet when planted to fill a border. They are long lasting and resistant to the weather. Not surprisingly, 'Purissima' has received the AGM.

GROUP Fosteriana
HEIGHT 45 cm (18 inches)
BLOOM TIME Mid-spring
CULTIVATION Full sun and deep, fertile, free-draining soil are needed to keep this bulb going, but like many Fosteriana tulips, it is remarkably adaptable.
LANDSCAPE AND DESIGN USES Not only are the flowers long lasting, the bulbs will persist in a border for many years, making it the perfect choice for permanent planting. Plant it so the flowers emerge with the young leaves of late-spring perennials like peonies and hardy geraniums. It also looks good with a backdrop of dark foliage such as low box or yew hedges in a formal parterre. Of course, it is an ideal bedding and container plant but don't skimp on the bulbs when you buy them. Plant densely and fill the border or pot to make the most impressive display.
ALTERNATIVES 'Sweetheart' has lemon-yellow flamed flowers edged with white and 'Purissima Design', a sport of 'Purissima', has variegated leaves with a yellow margin.

Tulipa 'Ivory Floradale'

From a silky, ivory white, oval bud, the huge blooms open to form a deep, wide bowl of rich creamy yellow. This tall, imposing tulip has a subtlety derived from the soft, dreamy colour of the broad petals. Introduced in 1965, it is a sport of the red 'Floradale' and it retains the dark anthers of that cultivar. Occasionally it has small red spots on the outer petals. I have seen this as a cut flower on the show bench at flower shows, and it really deserves all the attention it gets. It has received the AGM.

GROUP Darwin Hybrid

HEIGHT 60 cm (24 inches)

BLOOM TIME Mid-spring

CULTIVATION Despite its tall stems and large flowers, this tulip is remarkably weather resistant but I would still avoid growing it in very exposed locations.

LANDSCAPE AND DESIGN USES. It makes a wonderful bedding plant, especially when planted on its own in full sun and deep, fertile soil. If you plant it in a container, make it a large one and fit as many bulbs in as you can to get the best effect. It should also survive in a sunny, free-draining border without lifting but the size of the blooms will diminish over time.

ALTERNATIVES No other Darwin Hybrid has the same subtle blend of creamy white and pale yellow but you could try the pure white 'Hakuun', a new cultivar from Japan. Otherwise, you could substitute it with a yellow, such as 'Golden Apeldoorn' or the sport of it, 'Jaap Groot', which has a yellow flame over creamy white petals and white-edged foliage.

Tulipa 'Calgary'

The colour is similar to that of 'Purissima', with a faint yellow band up the centre of the ivory white petals. In 'Calgary' the white is brighter and more dominant, the flower smaller and squarer, and the stem shorter, making it an altogether more reserved tulip. It is short and sturdy, even for a Triumph tulip, and rigidly formal, making it ideal for bedding. The petals yellow towards the base inside the flower and surround orange-yellow anthers. A newer addition to the Triumph tulips, it was named in 1995 and received the AGM in the same year so its appeal must have been recognized straight away.

GROUP Triumph
HEIGHT 20 cm (8 inches)
BLOOM TIME Mid-spring
CULTIVATION The typical growing conditions for tulips suit this cultivar but the bulbs are best lifted for the summer.
LANDSCAPE AND DESIGN USES 'Calgary' makes a superb bedding plant but be careful not to mix it with taller tulips that flower at the same time; otherwise you will have an unbalanced display. It is better to plant it with other short spring bulbs, like blue anemones and *Muscari*, or traditional bedding plants like violas and polyanthus. The short stem means you can use a low container without it looking top heavy. Place a couple of pots of 'Calgary' either side of your back door to brighten up a porch or terrace.
ALTERNATIVES There are a few white Triumph tulips, such as 'White Dream' and 'Inzell', but they are taller than 'Calgary', reaching 40 to 50 cm (16 to 20 inches).

Tulipa 'White Triumphator'

This must be the height of sophistication in a tulip. The graceful lily-shaped flower is pure, unadulterated white and is held on a tall stem, bringing style and elegance to your garden. The pointed petals form a goblet-shaped bloom, with a flared rim as they arch back in the sun. Registered in 1942, this old cultivar is still widely used today and a favourite of many people. It has the AGM.

GROUP Lily-flowered
HEIGHT 60 cm (24 inches)
BLOOM TIME Mid to late spring
CULTIVATION Plant in a sunny position, where it will persist for a few years if the soil drains freely.
LANDSCAPE AND DESIGN USES A tall terracotta pot filled with this tulip makes a wonderful show. On its own, the purity of colour gives it a restrained elegance, but planting it with other tulips can provide some dramatic contrasts. The white flower can be mixed with a range of colours, from the dark purple Single Late 'Queen of Night' to the primrose yellow of Lily-flowered 'West Point' or the bi-coloured 'Claudia'. As well as containers and bedding, 'White Triumphator' looks good in a border or around the base of a tree.
ALTERNATIVES 'Très Chic' is another elegant, white Lily-flowered tulip, but it is shorter than 'White Triumphator' and has a touch of greenish yellow in the flower.

Tulipa 'Super Parrot'

With a name like 'Super Parrot', great things are expected of this tulip and if you want wild, flamboyant petals of luxurious ivory white with splashes of green, then you won't be disappointed. The green flicks up from the base on the outside of each petal and sprays out from the mid vein over the pure white background. The amount of green varies from flower to flower but all display the mad, irregular shape expected of the most extravagant Parrot tulips. This is a sport of the Triumph tulip 'White Dream' and was registered in 1996.

GROUP Parrot
HEIGHT 40 cm (16 inches)
BLOOM TIME Mid to late spring
CULTIVATION The splayed petals of the fully open flowers can be damaged by wind and rain so some shelter may be beneficial. The bulbs are unlikely to live long in a border if not lifted so plant new bulbs every year.
LANDSCAPE AND DESIGN USES Plant 'Super Parrot' in bedding, using it as a bright partner to darker tulips like 'Rococo' and 'Black Parrot'. It will complement the Viridiflora tulip 'Spring Green', both having white flowers marked with green, but a darker tulip mixed in will provide a welcome contrast and add depth of the display. Like most Parrot tulips, 'Super Parrot' makes a good container plant.
ALTERNATIVES 'White Parrot' makes a good alternative. It has pure white flowers, without prominent green markings, held in a more rounded bloom.

Tulipa 'Honeymoon'

This pure white tulip is most useful as a contrast to darker tulips but it also gives an unusual frosty look to bedding. The flower is a shallow cup holding pale yellow anthers and the petal margins are heavily cut to give the frosty, crystalline appearance that looks most effective when this tulip is planted in a group. A new addition to the Fringed range of tulips, 'Honeymoon' was registered in 2000.

GROUP Fringed
HEIGHT 45 cm (18 inches)
BLOOM TIME Mid to late spring
CULTIVATION Grow in full sun and free-draining soil but for the best display, plant new bulbs every year.
LANDSCAPE AND DESIGN USES This is a tulip for bedding or containers, where it can be mixed with other colours or planted on its own. The rich purple of 'Cuban Night' offset by the frosty white 'Honeymoon' is a striking combination that shows this tulip at its best, but try it with others in this group, like 'Red Hat' or 'Cummins'. Fill a container with just this tulip for a wonderfully crisp display.
ALTERNATIVES Other white Fringed tulips include the older cultivar 'Swan Wings', which is a little taller and has contrasting black anthers. The more recent 'Daytona' is very similar and can occasionally be found for sale.

Tulipa 'Spring Green'

The lovely, fresh-looking 'Spring Green' is a very popular tulip, probably because it is easy on the eye and presents few challenges. It is a simple flower shape and colour to mix with other tulips, and it grows a strong, upright stem that is resistant to wind. The flower is made up of creamy white petals that have a green flame up their centre and are slightly twisted to give an informal look. Inside the flower the green flame can be seen on the inner surface of the petals and there is no contrasting blotch. The anthers are pale green. This tulip dates from 1969 and has the AGM.

GROUP Viridiflora
HEIGHT 50 cm (20 inches)
BLOOM TIME Mid to late spring
CULTIVATION Find a sunny spot and deep, fertile soil that doesn't retain too much moisture in summer.
LANDSCAPE AND DESIGN USES I think this is a tulip to mix with other colours as it can look a little insipid on its own. Luckily, it is suited to a mixed border, complementing the fresh greens, pinks, blues, and yellows of spring perennials. In a container or bedding, underplant it with strongly coloured plants or mix it with the new Viridiflora tulips 'Yellow Spring Green' and 'Red Spring Green'.
ALTERNATIVES For something the same colour but a little different, try 'Greenstar'. It has the same white flowers with green flames as 'Spring Green', but the petals are pointed and arch back, like a Lily-flowered tulip.

Tulipa 'Angel's Wish'

This lovely tulip was bred in Latvia, registered in 2007, and a year later received the AGM. It is a similar colour to the Fosteriana tulip 'Purissima' but the flower is a little wider and forms a shallower cup. The stem is taller than that of 'Purissima' and the flower appears later in the season. The rounded petals are creamy white and the outer three have a prominent yellow, lance-shaped flame reaching up from the base that fades as the flower ages. Inside the flower is a small yellow central blotch. In the sunlight, the gleaming white blooms with their yellow flames make a lasting impression.

GROUP Single Late
HEIGHT 55 cm (22 inches)
BLOOM TIME Late spring
CULTIVATION This tulip does best in full sun and free-draining soil. Bulbs can be lifted for the summer, but it is best to plant new every year to maintain the uniformity of height and flower size this tulip has been bred to deliver.
LANDSCAPE AND DESIGN USES Few Single Late tulips can match 'Angel's Wish' for purity of colour, except perhaps the taller 'Maureen'. Although ideally suited to bedding, it is not too tall for a container. Combine it with a dark purple, like 'Queen of Night' or 'Recreado', which are similar heights.
ALTERNATIVES The taller, older, and more established 'Maureen' is the obvious alternative if you can't find 'Angel's Wish'.

Tulipa 'Maureen'

The oval flower of this statuesque tulip starts life with
a faint greenish yellow staining on the outer petals but
matures to gleaming white with just a hint of yellow. There
is an elegant simplicity to 'Maureen', with its unpreten-
tious, rounded white flower on a tall stem, late in the season. It is an old cultivar, dating from 1950, but has become
a favourite in the Single Late Group and is unsurpassed
even after all these years.

GROUP Single Late
HEIGHT 70 cm (28 inches)
BLOOM TIME Late spring
CULTIVATION Although very tall, this tulip is sturdy and can
withstand being planted in an exposed location. To maintain uniformity and impact, plant new bulbs every year.
LANDSCAPE AND DESIGN USES 'Maureen' is a bedding tulip
through and through, like many of the Single Late cultivars,
and it provides the boldness and uniformity of size and
height required for this purpose. Plant it under ornamental
cherry trees and the tulip will flower as the cherry blossom
rains down. Combine it with other tall tulips like pale pink
'Menton' or orange-pink 'Dordogne'.
ALTERNATIVES 'Clearwater' is a more modern cultivar
in the Single Late Group with a clear white flower and a
tall stem. Another alternative is the equally beautiful but
shorter 'Angel's Wish', which retains the hint of yellow that
gives the flower such depth of colour.

Tulipa humilis 'Albocaerulea Oculata'

This enchanting little tulip has a long name but a small white flower with a steely indigo blue centre. In some forms, this blotch is probably the closest to the elusive true blue you will find in any tulip. The stem is short so the star-shaped flower with its pointed petals is held close to the ground, just above the narrow leaves. It is a form of *Tulipa humilis* and comes from the eastern end of the natural range of that species, in northern Iran. It really needs a dry summer so cannot be left outside in most gardens, but with some protection from summer rain it will reward you with its remarkable and unique flower.

GROUP Miscellaneous
HEIGHT 10 cm (4 inches)
BLOOM TIME Early to mid-spring
CULTIVATION Unlike most forms of *T. humilis*, this one needs to be kept dry in summer so unless you can repli-cate its natural habitat in your garden you will have to grow it under glass. This will also protect the flower from the early spring weather, as rain and general dampness are not kind to this tulip. Use a gritty soil and let it dry out once the leaves have died down. Repot the bulbs in autumn and water them in to get growth going again.
LANDSCAPE AND DESIGN USES This tulip can be grown in a pot kept in a well-ventilated, cool conservatory or glass-house. The extra effort is worthwhile to see those rare blooms.
ALTERNATIVES There is no real alternative to this tulip. Other forms of *T. humilis* will be a similar size and have the same star-shaped flower but the colour of 'Albocaerulea Oculata' is out on its own.

Tulipa clusiana 'Lady Jane'

Beautifully slim and elegant, this tulip has a white flower painted with a broad brush of magenta pink on the back of the pointed outer petals. When the sun shines the flower opens wide to form a floppy, white star with a pale yellow centre and dark purple anthers, but when closed up the pink backs are put on show, looking like striped candy. The stem is slender but stiff and holds the flower above the long, narrow leaves. This is a vigorous form of the lady tulip (*Tulipa clusiana*) which grows wild from the eastern Himalaya to Iran and is naturalized further west in Turkey and southern Europe. The species can have white or yellow flowers, with a dark purple or pale yellow blotch inside the flower. 'Lady Jane' is one of several cultivars of this species and was named in 1992. It has an AGM.

GROUP Miscellaneous
HEIGHT 30 cm (12 inches)
BLOOM TIME Mid-spring
CULTIVATION Once planted, this tulip can be left in the ground to flower for several years. It thrives in a Mediterranean climate but will survive in wetter climates if grown in a sunny position and well-drained soil.
LANDSCAPE AND DESIGN USES 'Lady Jane' is not tall, so place it near the front of a border or grow it with smaller spring plants, like *Pulsatilla*, *Muscari*, or primroses. It is not a bedding plant but one for an informal border or rock garden. The pink-backed flowers look great whether open wide or closed up against the cold.
ALTERNATIVES *Tulipa clusiana* itself is shorter and has a dark centre to the flower but makes a good alternative. Another selection of the species, 'Peppermintstick', is taller and more intensely coloured, with a dark centre and rose pink outer petals. It also has an AGM.

Tulipa turkestanica

One bulb of this multi-flowered species can produce up to 12 small white flowers. Each flower may be small, but the effect of them opening at the same time on the branching stem is mesmerizing. The pointed petals are white but at the centre of the flower is a bright yellow blotch. It reminds me of a nest of baby birds all facing upwards with their beaks open. The species comes from Central Asia, where it grows wild in the mountains of the Pamir Alai and Tien Shan. It was described by the great Russian botanist Eduard Regel in 1875. Although this is a variable species, the form in general cultivation is surprisingly adaptable to garden conditions and well worth finding space for. It has received the AGM.

GROUP Miscellaneous
HEIGHT 20 cm (8 inches)
BLOOM TIME Early to mid-spring
CULTIVATION It needs full sun and well-drained soil but you don't have to restrict it to the driest part of the garden, as it can do well in normal border conditions, as long as the soil is not too heavy and wet, and the flowers are not smothered by taller plants.
LANDSCAPE AND DESIGN USES Scatter the bulbs through a sunny border, gravel garden, or raised bed so they grow through low perennials and provide a little sparkle in late winter or early spring. Plant several bulbs together to maximize the effect of those clustered, glistening blooms.
ALTERNATIVES A number of tulips have small white flowers with a yellow centre but the closest to *T. turkestanica* in size and number of blooms is *T. bifloriformis*. Its selection 'Starlight' also has the AGM.

Tulipa urumiensis

SYNONYM *Tulipa tarda*

Bulbs sold as *T. tarda* are among the last of the tulip species to bloom, producing bright, flat, starry flowers with a broad yellow centre. This yellow blotch covers a large part of the flower, leaving just the tips of the petals white. The species is now properly named *T. urumiensis*, an older name first used to describe forms with completely yellow flowers from Iran, but the name *T. tarda* is more often used in cultivation and under this name it has received the AGM. Either way, it is an attractive garden tulip, with each bulb growing several narrow leaves and short stems holding up to eight flowers clustered close to the ground.

GROUP Miscellaneous
HEIGHT 10 cm (4 inches)
BLOOM TIME Late spring
CULTIVATION Good drainage and full sun suit it best, but it can be grown in normal, open-textured garden soil.
LANDSCAPE AND DESIGN USES With its leaves and flowers being held so close to the ground, the best place to grow this small tulip is a gravel garden or rock garden, where the rosette of leaves can rest on the gravel mulch to keep them dry and prevent them being splashed by soil. I've said this about other small tulips, but you really need to make sure this one isn't swamped by surrounding plants.
ALTERNATIVES Plants sold as *T. urumiensis* have entirely yellow flowers but are otherwise very similar, and it also has the AGM. For white flowers with a yellow centre, any of the species related to *T. biflora* can be planted, such as those sold under the name *T. polychroma*, but they are taller.

YELLOW

Bright, luminous yellow—the colour of spring, of sunshine, and of daffodils—is also the colour of a range of gorgeous tulips. From deep golden yellow, through primrose yellow to pale lemon yellow, these tulips bring warmth and vitality to the spring garden. Some have petals backed with a flash of red or have feathers and flames reaching up from the base of the flower, but the overall effect is of dazzling, sunny yellow.

Tulipa 'Stresa'

'Stresa' is a bright and early tulip with a predominantly yellow flower that forms a broad cup on a short stem, opening up to a star in the sun. The outer three petals have a bold red band on the back, like a triangle reaching from the base to the pointed tip, leaving only the petal margins yellow. The inner three petals have just a thin red line up the centre. Inside, the flower is yellow, apart from red markings towards the throat, near the long, thin yellow anthers. The leaves are mottled, which shows the influence of *T. greigii* in its breeding, but the shape of the flower and its early appearance puts this tulip firmly in the Kaufmanniana Group. It was registered in 1942 and has the AGM.

GROUP Kaufmanniana
HEIGHT 25 cm (10 inches)
BLOOM TIME Early spring
CULTIVATION Good drainage and a sunny location provide the perfect conditions, and here it may survive and flower for several years. A little dappled shade will encourage the stems of the tulip to grow a bit taller.
LANDSCAPE AND DESIGN USES This tulip can be used for bedding out if you want early flowers and it is even better in a container, where it will bring some early spring cheer. It can be grown in a gravel garden, rock garden, or raised bed. The large flowers on a short stem can look out of place in naturalistic planting scheme, so place it carefully, maybe poking through foliage or around the base of a shrub.
ALTERNATIVES In the Kaufmanniana Group, 'Giuseppe Verdi' (see photo on page 62) has golden yellow flowers with red on the outer surface of the outer three petals, and red markings inside the flower.

Tulipa 'Mickey Mouse'

This is a cheerful tulip and with a name like 'Mickey Mouse' it should be. Deep red flames spread up the golden yellow petals. The flames vary, with some petals displaying a broad splash of red at their base that reaches up to the tip, while on other petals the flame is a narrow spear with wisps of red spreading outwards over the yellow background. The red flames are just as strong inside the flower, but there is a yellow zone at the centre and small purple anthers. Registered in 1960, it is sport of the deep lemon yellow 'Wintergold'. It may not be the most sophisticated or subtle tulip, but it should bring a smile to your face.

GROUP Single Early
HEIGHT 35 cm (14 inches)
BLOOM TIME Early to mid-spring
CULTIVATION The usual growing conditions of fertile, free-draining soil are fine for this tulip.
LANDSCAPE AND DESIGN USES Although the cup-shaped flower is on the small side, a group of them makes a bright and uplifting show, so plant up a container or group it together in bedding to make the most of its cheery blooms. Like most Single Early tulips, the shorter stem is an advantage when it comes to putting up with windy conditions. I prefer it on its own rather than mixed with other tulips.
ALTERNATIVES The Single Early tulip 'Keizerskroon' is a very old cultivar, dating from 1750, and has yellow flowers with a broad red fan on each yellow petal.

Tulipa 'Monte Carlo'

Individually, the flower of this tulip looks a bit shambolic, but grouped in a container or bedding display the strong colour and long-lasting double blooms have an impact that is not reliant on the weather. The short stem holds a bunch of deep sulphur yellow petals that form an open head, starting out as a broad cup and gradually becoming looser and more ruffled as the flower ages. The attributes of this cultivar have been appreciated for many years and it is still often grown despite being around for over sixty years. It has the AGM.

GROUP Double Early

HEIGHT 30 cm (12 inches)

BLOOM TIME Mid-spring

CULTIVATION Grow this tulip in full sun and well-drained soil. The heavy flowers can bend the stem in rain or wind.

LANDSCAPE AND DESIGN USES This is definitely a plant for formal bedding, as it is hard to use in a mixed border without it looking out of place. There is nothing worse than a subtle display of spring perennials interrupted by clumps of artificial-looking tulips scattered through the planting. However, in the right place 'Monte Carlo' has plenty to give. Fill a container or group it together with other bedding plants to create a bold and reliable design that will bring colour to the garden for several weeks.

ALTERNATIVES 'Monsella' is a sport of 'Monte Carlo' and has yellow double blooms with feathers of red on the outside. For a softer, more subtle yellow try 'Montreux'.

Tulipa 'Montreux'

The flower of this double tulip is similar in shape and form to 'Monte Carlo' but it is held on a taller stem and, more significantly, is a softer, paler yellow. It's amazing how the colour can make such a difference. 'Montreux' isn't a better tulip than 'Monte Carlo', but the more subtle hue gives it a completely different character—not strong and bold but fragile and more discreet. The colour is pale primrose yellow, deeper inside the flower and fading towards the petal margins. It sits somewhere between 'Monte Carlo' and the silky, creamy white of 'Verona'.

GROUP Double Early
HEIGHT 45 cm (18 inches)
BLOOM TIME Mid-spring
CULTIVATION Although double flowers don't need the warmth of the sun to open, they still need a sunny position to do well and keep them strong and healthy.
LANDSCAPE AND DESIGN USES 'Montreux' has a colour that goes best with pale bedding plants such as the light blue *Muscari* 'Peppermint', which is how I saw it planted at Keukenhof. A combination that is well worth trying is mixing it with the pale 'Verona' and the strong yellow 'Monte Carlo'. All three of these double tulips would work well together, creating an undulating carpet in varying shades of yellow.
ALTERNATIVES In the Double Early Group, 'Verona' and 'Monte Carlo' are the obvious alternatives, both providing a different shade of the same colour.

Tulipa 'Sweetheart'

In a group of tulips renowned for their large, vivid, single-coloured flowers, this cultivar is unusual and distinctive. Not all Fosteriana tulips are bright red, orange, or yellow; there are notable exceptions, like the wonderful 'Flaming Purissima'. In 'Sweetheart' the flower is patterned with flames of lemon yellow reaching up from the base, leaving just an ivory white edge, inside and out. From a distance the effect created by a group of this tulip is a cloud of pale, creamy yellow, but closer inspection reveals the wisps and flares dancing up the side of the wide petals.

GROUP Fosteriana

HEIGHT 40 cm (16 inches)

BLOOM TIME Mid-spring

CULTIVATION Given good drainage and a sunny position, it can be left in the ground to continue flowering for several years.

LANDSCAPE AND DESIGN USES Like the pure white 'Purissima', 'Sweetheart' makes a very effective bedding plant. The bright flowers add a glowing quality to any design. Underplant with white *Anemone blanda* or yellow violas, or mix it with later daffodils like the yellow *Narcissus* 'Quail'. Enhance the white in the tulip with the pheasant's eye, *N. poeticus*. This tulip will also do well in an informal setting, growing with spring perennials in a mixed border.

ALTERNATIVES For a stronger yellow you could use 'Yellow Purissima' or 'Golden Emperor' and for white there is always 'Purissima'.

Tulipa 'Daydream'

Aging beautifully, the flower, which begins as a pure yellow bowl, develops into a wide plate of pale orange with contrasting black anthers and a small greenish black blotch at the centre. The orange colour first appears near the middle of each broad, rounded petal and spreads towards the margins, leaving the base of the petal yellow around the small dark blotch. The flower is large, and in a group of this tulip there will be a delicious mix of yellows and oranges, varying in intensity. This cultivar was registered in 1980 and is a sport of 'Yellow Dover', itself a sport of the red-flowered 'Dover'. 'Daydream' has a well-deserved AGM.

GROUP Darwin Hybrid
HEIGHT 55 cm (22 inches)
BLOOM TIME Mid-spring
CULTIVATION Plant in sun and deep, fertile, well-drained garden soil for the best results.
LANDSCAPE AND DESIGN USES The sunny yellow and orange tones of this tulip are suited to bedding or more informal planting. It looks best on its own instead of mixed with other tulips so you can make the most of the varying shades it provides. I have grown it in a mixed border under a weeping cherry tree and the flowers appeared along with the pale pink cherry blossom, which clung to the drooping branches and mixed with the tulip's colourful bloom. In this position it received plenty of sunshine before the leaves unfurled on the tree. The soil was far from ideal, being heavy clay, but even here this tulip flowered for a couple of years.
ALTERNATIVES 'American Dream' is a sport of 'Daydream' and a much deeper orange but still with the yellow centre to the flower. 'Golden Apeldoorn', a sport of red 'Apeldoorn', is a deep golden yellow.

Tulipa 'Golden Parade'

A great, egg-shaped flower of buttercup yellow held on a tall stem with broad, grey-green leaves makes an impressive sight, even compared to other Darwin Hybrids. The flower is pure yellow apart from a very fine and delicate margin of red that picks out the shape of the wide, rounded petals against the yellow background. Registered in 1963, it is a sport of the red 'Parade'. This tulip has a great presence in the garden, flowering mid-season with bowls of glowing yellow that open in the sun to reveal a small black blotch inside the flower and black anthers.

GROUP Darwin Hybrid
HEIGHT 60 cm (24 inches)
BLOOM TIME Mid-spring
CULTIVATION As for other Darwin Hybrids, sun and fertile, well-drained soil suit this tulip best.
LANDSCAPE AND DESIGN USES This is an imposing tulip, whether planted in a border or bedding. Plant it under deciduous trees to take over the spring display of yellow from early daffodils or mix with later white daffodils, like *Narcissus poeticus*, that will flower at the same time. Once in leaf, the trees will keep the soil dry for the summer and the tulip will return to bloom again if left in the ground.
ALTERNATIVES 'Golden Apeldoorn' has a similar, large yellow flower on a tall stem.

Tulipa 'Olympic Flame'

Flames of scarlet flick up the sides of this showy, yellow tulip. The amount of red varies from petal to petal, with some having just a few flashes along the margin and others displaying a broad red flare up the centre, reaching the rounded tip. The flames show both on the inside and outside of the flower and the anthers are black. This cultivar is a sport of deep buttercup yellow 'Olympic Gold', which is a sport of 'Lefeber's Favourite', a deep red tulip. The red didn't show up in 'Olympic Gold' but has made a welcome comeback in this flashy cultivar, which was registered in 1971 and has the AGM.

GROUP Darwin Hybrid
HEIGHT 55 cm (22 inches)
BLOOM TIME Mid-spring
CULTIVATION In a sunny, well-drained site it should do well without the need to lift the bulbs for the summer.
LANDSCAPE AND DESIGN USES Plant 'Olympic Flame' in bedding or a container for a glitzy show in mid-spring. Try it in a border or under deciduous trees, maybe mixed with 'Golden Parade' for a lavish display.
ALTERNATIVES Another yellow Darwin Hybrid with flames of red is 'Burning Heart', but the petals are a paler, creamy yellow, fading to creamy white as they age.

Tulipa 'Limelight'

This enigmatic tulip has a flower of wonderful soft, pale, luminous yellow. There are no contrasting petal margins, flames, or feathers to mar the purity of colour found in this cultivar. It is an old tulip and not widely available, but if you come across it you will be struck by the simplicity and clarity of its flowers.

GROUP Triumph

HEIGHT 50 cm (20 inches)

BLOOM TIME Mid-spring

CULTIVATION The usual growing conditions are appropriate but lift the bulbs to ensure they have a dry summer.

LANDSCAPE AND DESIGN USES The colour is probably a little too subtle to plant on its own in bedding but it makes a beautiful container plant. A combination I haven't tried but worth considering is pairing it with 'Candy Prince'. Both tulips have that soft, luminous quality to their flowers—'Limelight' in yellow and 'Candy Prince' in pale purple. The latter is a Single Early tulip so will flower earlier, but for a time both tulips will bloom together before the purple fades away and the yellow takes over.

ALTERNATIVES Yellows in the Triumph Group include the lemon yellow 'Lady Margot', the tall 'Francoise', and the rich yellow, sturdy and aptly named 'Strong Gold'.

Tulipa 'Synaeda King'

The flower is a fiery combination of canary yellow marked with a broad slash of bright orange-red reaching up from the base on the outside of the petals. On the outer three petals, the red stretches all the way up to the long pointed tip but on the inner three it stops short, leaving a wide yellow margin. Inside the flower there is a red patch on each petal but the base is pure yellow, with dark blackish brown anthers. The colour of this tulip could be called red, orange, or yellow, but I think yellow is the more dominant colour overall, especially when the flower opens up in the sun. The cultivar was registered in 1995 and has the AGM.

GROUP Lily-flowered
HEIGHT 50 cm (20 inches)
BLOOM TIME Mid to late spring
CULTIVATION Planted in sun and fertile, free-draining soil, it may survive to flower again without lifting.
LANDSCAPE AND DESIGN USES Plant up a large pot of this tulip for a sunny patio or terrace. It will give any spot in the garden a lift with its sizzling colours. It is great for bedding of course, planted in a large group, or mixed with other tulips like the pure yellow 'West Point' or the orange 'Ballerina', which are also Lily-flowered and will complement the colours in 'Synaeda King'.
ALTERNATIVES 'Fly Away' is a more recently bred Lily-flowered tulip with similar colours, although there is a larger area of red on the outside of the flower, leaving just a narrow yellow margin to the petals.

Tulipa 'West Point'

This simple tulip has a single bright colour that emphasizes the elegant shape of the flower. The pure primrose yellow petals are drawn out into a long, slender point and they arch back when fully open in the sun. When closed up, the petals are held tight together, giving the flower the typical narrow waist of the Lily-flowered tulips. 'West Point' is a popular and well-established cultivar that dates from 1943 and has received the AGM.

GROUP Lily-flowered
HEIGHT 50 cm (20 inches)
BLOOM TIME Mid to late spring
CULTIVATION In a sunny position and well-drained soil, the bulb can survive without lifting and will flower again, brightening up a dull corner with its sunny, fluted blooms.
LANDSCAPE AND DESIGN USES Plant in bedding on its own or with other tulips for a colour scheme of your choice. Mix with 'White Triumphator' for a yellow and white design or 'Merlot' for purple and yellow; the possibilities are many and varied. 'West Point' can also be used in a mixed border.
ALTERNATIVES There are a few yellow Lily-flowered tulips, including 'Moonshine', 'Moonlight Girl', and 'Flashback'.

Tulipa 'Yellow Spring Green'

In the same way that 'Red Spring Green' has a distinctive flower, 'Yellow Spring Green' is another tulip in the same group that stands out due the combination of a bright base colour and subdued green highlights on a well-proportioned plant. It is a sport of the popular 'Spring Green', and these new variations on that classic tulip are a step in the right direction in tulip breeding as far as I'm concerned. 'Yellow Spring Green' has a rich, greenish yellow flower, with a wide band of green up the centre of each petal. The pale pink anthers add an interesting contrast to the rest of the flower.

GROUP Viridiflora

HEIGHT 50 cm (20 inches)

BLOOM TIME Late spring

CULTIVATION Plant in fertile, free-draining soil and full sun. To encourage repeat flowering in subsequent years, it is best to lift the bulbs and store them cool and dry until autumn

LANDSCAPE AND DESIGN USES This cultivar is best used in a container or bedding scheme, either on its own or with other late spring tulips. The bright yellow adds an enlightening glow and, in combination with the more restrained green markings, means this tulip mixes especially well with blue flowers, such as *Muscari* or forget-me-nots (*Myosotis*).

ALTERNATIVES *Tulipa* 'Formosa' has a similarly coloured flower but of a deeper yellow, and the petals are longer and more pointed than in 'Yellow Spring Green'.

Tulipa 'Big Smile'

There is nothing complicated about this tulip, just a big, jolly, yellow flower on a tall stem in late spring. It does a good job of being simply big and yellow, and a group of these flowers may well bring a smile to your face. The deep lemon yellow petals form a deep, narrow cup-shaped bloom from an egg-shaped bud. This strong and imposing tulip excels in bedding and was registered in 1990.

GROUP Single Late
HEIGHT 60 cm (24 inches)
BLOOM TIME Late spring
CULTIVATION The usual conditions of sun and well-drained soil are needed by this imposing tulip.
LANDSCAPE AND DESIGN USES Bred to provide a bright yellow flower in late spring, 'Big Smile' is the perfect bedding tulip. Plant on its own for a broad sweep of yellow or mix with other tall Single Late tulips like the creamy white 'Maureen' and 'Angel's Wish' or the reddish purple 'Renown'. Like the Lily-flowered 'West Point', this single-coloured tulip can be mixed with a whole range of colours to create what-ever effect you desire.
ALTERNATIVES The classic yellow Single Late tulip is the much older 'Mrs John T. Scheepers', which has been described as the best yellow tulip ever. Maybe it's time 'Big Smile' took over that crown.

Tulipa acuminata

This remarkable tulip has exquisitely narrow, sinuous petals that form a pointed flower reminiscent of the exotic-looking needle tulips depicted in eighteenth-century Ottoman art. The origin of this tulip is uncertain but it is undoubtedly a hybrid with a long history in cultivation. It was given its current name in 1813, when it appeared in a list of plants growing in Copenhagen Botanic Garden. The colour varies from plant to plant, with some having almost pure yellow flowers and just a few streaks of red to those with much heavier red staining over the yellow base colour. The petals are held close together to form the evocative, needle-shaped flower, but in the sun they open out to create a fascinating, spidery bloom.

GROUP Miscellaneous
HEIGHT 40 cm (16 inches)
BLOOM TIME Mid-spring
CULTIVATION Plant in sun or lightly dappled shade. The bulb will survive summer in the ground as long as the soil is well drained.
LANDSCAPE AND DESIGN USES Grown for intrigue and novelty rather than pure display, this tulip has a mysterious elegance unmatched by other spring bulbs. Plant it in a mixed border and imagine your garden is in the grounds of Istanbul's Topkapi Palace, overlooking the Bosporus and basking in the Mediterranean sun. This tulip will do well peering through the fresh foliage of newly emerging herbaceous perennials.
ALTERNATIVES There is no alternative to this unique tulip. The closest you will get is one of the more spidery Lily-flowered tulips but they have relatively substantial flowers that provide more of a show but lack the finesse of *T. acuminata*.

Tulipa clusiana var. *chrysantha*

This yellow form of the lady tulip has bright sunny flowers with a broad band of crimson up the outside of the outer petals, leaving a narrow yellow margin. When the flower is tightly closed, the crimson backs of the petals are displayed but as it opens up, the petals spread wide in the warmth of the sun and they expose their deep golden yellow inner surface. The inner three petals are entirely yellow, darker towards the base, and they surround the yellow anthers. The flower is held on a short, slender stem above the narrow blue-green leaves. This tulip grows wild in Central Asia but is well established in cultivation and has the AGM.

GROUP Miscellaneous
HEIGHT 25 cm (10 inches)
BLOOM TIME Mid-spring
CULTIVATION Grow in a sunny position. The bulb needs to be dry in summer but will survive left in the ground if the soil drains freely. In such a site it will continue to flower every spring.
LANDSCAPE AND DESIGN USES A sunny border in a gravel garden, rock garden, or raised bed is most suitable for this tulip. It is not tall, so be careful not to smother it with plants that are more vigorous. It can also be grown in a container so find a terracotta pot and fit in as many bulbs as you can. Give the pot some shelter, in a cold frame or cool glasshouse, until the flower buds appear and then bring it out to a sunny spot in the garden to enjoy those pretty blooms. You can also mix it with a range of small spring bulbs, like smaller daffodils or different tulip species.
ALTERNATIVES This yellow form of *T. clusiana* is often more widely available than the white form but there are several cultivars that would make good alternatives, such as 'Tubergen's Gem' and the paler, primrose yellow 'Tinka'.

Tulipa 'Honky Tonk'

This dainty tulip has pale yellow flowers flushed with a hint of red on the outer petals. Although sometimes listed as a cultivar of *Tulipa linifolia* Batalinii Group, it is closer to *T. clusiana* in size and form in my opinion. The flower is a narrow cup but as it opens up the outer petals arch back leaving the inner three more upright. Ultimately the inner three petals will arch back as well to make an open bloom. Inside, the flower is all yellow and has slender, dark brown anthers. The inner petals are a deeper yellow than the outer three, which are quite pale, especially towards their pointed tips. The amount of red on the outside of the petals varies but is never as strong as is found on yellow forms of *T. clusiana*. 'Honky Tonk' is a hybrid, introduced in 1998, and it has the AGM.

GROUP Miscellaneous
HEIGHT 20 cm (8 inches)
BLOOM TIME Mid-spring
CULTIVATION Like *T. clusiana* and *T. linifolia*, this tulip needs a sunny position and free-draining soil. It can survive left in the ground if the soil is not too wet in summer.
LANDSCAPE AND DESIGN USES Grow it in a gravel garden, raised bed, or rock garden, alongside other small bulbs or alpines, or plant it near the front of a mixed border where it won't be hidden from view. It also makes a great pot plant, brought out from the shelter of a cold frame or cool glasshouse when the buds emerge from between the grey-green leaves and placed on a sunny patio or terrace.
ALTERNATIVES The yellow forms of *T. clusiana* are similar but a little taller and with a prominent red band on the outer petals. Yellow forms of *T. linifolia* tend to be shorter but they do have pure yellow flowers, with a hint of pink, bronze, or orange.

Tulipa dasystemon

This small species is closely related to *T. tarda* and has completely yellow flowers and glossy, mid-green leaves. In the wild in Central Asia it can grow at altitudes up to 3200 m (10,500 feet) but forms from lower altitudes are easier to grow in the garden. These low-altitude forms are slightly taller and have been named *T. neustruevae*, a species now included within *T. dasystemon*. The deep golden yellow flowers are backed with bronzy brown on the outer petals and there can be two or three on each plant. The flower is globe-like as it opens but in the warmth the petals will bend back to form a flat star that revels in the spring sunshine.

GROUP Miscellaneous
HEIGHT 15 cm (6 inches)
BLOOM TIME Mid-spring
CULTIVATION It needs sun and good drainage, with a mulch of grit around the plant to keep the leaves and flowers away from wet soil. Bulbs should be left in the ground where they will naturally increase to form a slowly spreading group.
LANDSCAPE AND DESIGN USES A small tulip but with a bunch of rich yellow flowers that brightens up a spring border. It is best grown on a rock garden or the edge of a border in a gravel garden.
ALTERNATIVES *Tulipa urumiensis* also has star-like yellow flowers but on an even shorter plant. It requires similar conditions to *T. dasystemon*.

Tulipa linifolia Batalinii Group 'Bright Gem'

The bright little flower is held on a short stem just above the narrow blue-green leaves. The yellow forms of this species were previously called *Tulipa batalinii* but they are now considered just colour forms of *T. linifolia* and the cultivars are distinguished by naming them *T. linifolia* Batalinii Group. 'Bright Gem' has sulphur yellow blooms flushed with orange especially along the mid-vein of each pointed petal. Registered in 1952, it has long been a popular tulip and it has the AGM.

GROUP Miscellaneous
HEIGHT 15 cm (6 inches)
BLOOM TIME Mid-spring
CULTIVATION When grown in free-draining soil, it is reliably perennial and can be left in the ground to flower every spring.
LANDSCAPE AND DESIGN USES This tulip is neither extravagant nor flashy, but its understated, softly coloured flowers add a bright spot to a sunny rock garden, raised bed, or gravel garden. It can also be grown in a small pot, just like the other species, protected in a cold frame or cool glasshouse until ready to flower, when it can be brought out on show.
ALTERNATIVES Similar cultivars of *T. linifolia* include 'Apricot Jewel, 'Yellow Jewel', and 'Bronze Charm', which are all shades of yellow, delicately flushed with orange-red, rose pink, or bronze.

Tulipa mauritiana 'Cindy'

This tulip has rich primrose yellow flowers delicately feathered with red along the margins of the petals. The red colouring begins as a faint smudge along the petal edges but gradually spreads inwards as the flower ages. The usual form of *Tulipa mauritiana* has red flowers with a yellow base and is one of the neo-tulips, so-called species that have escaped from cultivation and turned up in parts of Europe, particularly among the foothills of the Alps in southeastern France. This tulip was found near the town of St. Jean-de-Maurienne in the Savoy region and named in 1858. In 'Cindy', a particularly desirable form named in 1979, the yellow base has spread to cover most of the flower.

GROUP Miscellaneous
HEIGHT 45 cm (18 inches)
BLOOM TIME Late spring
CULTIVATION This tulip doesn't need the free-draining, gritty soil that many other tulips require in the garden, making it one of the better tulips for general border conditions.
LANDSCAPE AND DESIGN USES Perfect for the edge of a woodland border, in lightly dappled shade, it flowers as the leaves of the trees unfurl. It can be grown among other spring woodlanders like *Erythronium* and anemones. The leafy trees will take excess moisture out of the soil so it should not be too wet in summer.
ALTERNATIVES All the neo-tulips can be grown in similar conditions and the closest in colour to 'Cindy' are *T. grengiolensis*, which has varying amounts of red along the petal margins, and the pale yellow *T. marjoletii*.

ORANGE

Mixing red and yellow together produces the warm glow of orange. There is no pure orange, just shades that vary between almost red to very near yellow. In between these two extremes are shades ranging from rich terracotta to pale, almost pastel hues. Several of the following tulips have red marks or staining over a yellow background, but these two separate colours combine in the flower to give the overall effect of orange.

Tulipa 'Early Harvest'

This is one of the earliest tulip cultivars to bloom and the petals display an enticing mix of colours. They are pinkish red on the outside and orange-red inside with a narrow yellow margin. The base of the flower is yellow, but this is mostly covered by a bronzy green smudge. The long thin anthers are also yellow. The funnel-shaped bloom opens up to form a waterlily shape in the sun, if it makes an appearance in early spring, and is held on a short stem between leaves that are grey-green with attractive purple markings, showing the influence of *T. greigii* in its breeding. 'Early Harvest' dates from 1955 and has the AGM. It's a great start to the tulip season.

GROUP Kaufmanniana
HEIGHT 25 cm (10 inches)
BLOOM TIME Early spring
CULTIVATION In a sunny site, with fertile, free-draining soil, this tulip can be left in the ground to flower every spring. If used as bedding then any good garden soil is fine.
LANDSCAPE AND DESIGN USES Grow it in a mixed border or gravel garden to provide a bright and early display of colour. It is an early flower for bedding and can also be grown in a container.
ALTERNATIVES The Kaufmanniana tulip 'Love Song' has vivid, deep orange flowers and 'Shakespeare' has a salmon pink to orange-red flower.

Tulipa 'Love Song'

The combination of a vivid, orange-red flower held above broad leaves heavily marked with dark stripes is especially striking. Like 'Early Harvest', this tulip blooms early in the season, before most perennials are showing much above ground. The influence of *T. kaufmanniana* is seen in the starry, waterlily-like bloom that opens wide in the sun above its distinctive, striped foliage. The flower is held on a short stem and opens close to the ground, with wide, pointed petals surrounding thick yellow anthers. The stem elongates as spring progresses, pushing the gradually fading bloom through other emerging plants if grown in a mixed border.

GROUP Kaufmanniana
HEIGHT 25 cm (10 inches)
BLOOM TIME Early spring
CULTIVATION Well-drained, fertile soil and full sun are required to keep this tulip going for more than one year if left in the ground, but any good garden soil is fine if the bulbs are lifted or just used for an early spring bedding display.
LANDSCAPE AND DESIGN USES The early flowers are ideal for spring bedding but this tulip can be grown in a mixed border and looks great in a gravel garden, surrounded by other drought-tolerant perennials, such as lavender and sage. Try it in a container, too.
ALTERNATIVES 'Early Harvest' has deep orange petals that fade to yellow at the edges. Another early Kaufmanniana is the bright red 'Showwinner'.

Tulipa 'Flair'

Petals of deep golden yellow are flamed and feathered with red and orange inside and out in this striking early tulip. This is one of those tulips that glows when the sun shines through the flower and the variation in patterning gives the colour depth. Inside there is a dark blue-black blotch at the centre edged with a yellow margin. This compact tulip, little over 30 cm (12 inches) tall, is the perfect container plant. It was first registered in 1978 and although not commonly available now, it is worth searching out.

GROUP Single Early
HEIGHT 35 cm (14 inches)
BLOOM TIME Early to mid-spring
CULTIVATION Well-drained soil and bright sun are important for this tulip to thrive in the garden and it may survive a few years without lifting.
LANDSCAPE AND DESIGN USES Plant in a large container with small spring bulbs, like white *Anemone blanda* or small daffodils, and place it so it catches any early spring sunshine. It also makes a strong bedding plant and can be grown in a mixed border.
ALTERNATIVES 'Generaal de Wet' is an old Single Early tulip, dating from 1904; it has orange flowers stippled with red.

Tulipa 'Cape Cod'

There is nothing subtle about this tulip. The bright flower displays a mixture of yellow, orange, and red and looking straight down into it is like gazing into a kaleidoscope. The outer petals are deep orange, darkening to red near the base, with a yellow margin. The inner petals have a wider yellow margin, leaving a band of orange up the centre, reaching the tip. Inside the flower there is a black base, with yellow anthers, and a band of red up each yellow petal, giving that kaleidoscopic effect. The blue-green leaves have stripes and spots of purple.

GROUP Greigii
HEIGHT 30 cm (12 inches)
BLOOM TIME Mid-spring
CULTIVATION In the gritty, free-draining soil of a gravel garden it should survive the summer without lifting.
LANDSCAPE AND DESIGN USES This brightly coloured tulip is best planted in a container or bedded out. It's a little too dazzling to mix with more subtle flowers in a spring border.
ALTERNATIVES 'Quebec' has scarlet flowers with pale yellow margins to the petals and the new cultivar 'City Flower' has red petals edged with orange yellow.

Tulipa 'Orange Emperor'

This orange form of the impressive *T. fosteriana* is a colourful and resilient tulip, good for a range of garden situations. The large, funnel-shaped flower has broad petals of carrot orange with a yellow base. The amount of yellow varies from flower to flower and in some reaches in a lance shape almost to the petal tip. The wide, blue-green leaves are typical of this group. This tulip dates from 1962 but is still widely available, probably because there is nothing to compete with it. If you want an orange Fosteriana tulip, then this is the one. It has the AGM.

GROUP Fosteriana
HEIGHT 40 cm (16 inches)
BLOOM TIME Mid-spring
CULTIVATION Grow in sunshine and soil that isn't too wet in summer but it is an adaptable plant that can tolerate less than ideal conditions.
LANDSCAPE AND DESIGN USES I planted bulbs of 'Orange Emperor' in a remote corner of the garden, where they flowered for a few years and then I forgot about them. The corner became neglected, swamped with long grass and thistles, but ten years later I was amazed to find these tulips still blooming. This resilience makes 'Orange Emperor' a great choice for naturalizing in a mixed border. In a more formal setting it combines well with other Fosteriana tulips, especially 'Purissima', and later daffodils like *Narcissus* 'Cherry Spot', which has an orange corona to match the tulip.
ALTERNATIVES There are many tulips in this group, in a variety of colours, but 'Orange Emperor' seems to be the only orange on offer. For alternative large orange flowers, it is better to look at the Darwin Hybrid Group.

Tulipa 'Blushing Apeldoorn'

Take some of the best features of the Darwin Hybrid tulips, put them together in one plant and you have this magnificent cultivar. The large flower, the bright colour, and the petals finely highlighted with a narrow contrasting margin are all here. It may not be as refined as 'World's Favourite' or as effortlessly elegant as 'Ivory Floradale', but it has impact and charisma. The flower is yellow, heavily stained with orange reaching up from the base of the petals. The petals have a thin orange-red margin and inside the flower is a dark central blotch. Registered in 1989, 'Blushing Apeldoorn' is a sport of 'Beauty of Apeldoorn', which is a sport of 'Apeldoorn'.

GROUP Darwin Hybrid

HEIGHT 55 cm (22 inches)

BLOOM TIME Mid-spring

CULTIVATION Plant in sun, where it will flower every spring if the soil is fertile and well drained.

LANDSCAPE AND DESIGN USES This tulip adds rich, vibrant colour to bedding or you can plant it in a wide pot displayed on a sunny patio or terrace. Scatter bulbs under deciduous trees or through a sunny mixed border.

ALTERNATIVES There are several orange and yellow tulips in the Darwin Hybrid Group, including 'Daydream', 'American Dream', and 'Lightning Sun'.

Tulipa 'American Dream'

This sport of 'Daydream' has the same wide, saucer-shaped flower as its parent but in a dark, almost red, shade of orange. The base of each petal is yellow, forming a bright sunny centre to the flower, with a small, dark greenish black blotch and black anthers. The yellow spreads up the centre of each petal but soon gives way to the rich orange glow, which reaches its darkest towards the petal tip. The yellow colouring is more prominent on the outside of the petals, and when the bud is closed, it could be mistaken for a pale yellow flower. However, when fully open, this is a glorious, strong, large-flowered tulip.

GROUP Darwin Hybrid
HEIGHT 55 cm (22 inches)
BLOOM TIME Mid-spring
CULTIVATION In good free-draining soil and full sun it will persist in the garden, like many in this flamboyant group of tulips.
LANDSCAPE AND DESIGN USES Like 'Daydream' this tulip is suited to both formal bedding schemes and informal, mixed plantings. Combine it with other tall Darwin Hybrids, like 'Golden Parade' or 'Olympic Flame'.
ALTERNATIVES Darwin Hybrid tulips with orange flowers include 'Apeldoorn's Elite', the yellow to pale orange 'Daydream', and the wonderful 'Blushing Apeldoorn'.

Tulipa 'Prinses Irene'

'Prinses Irene' is a lovely, compact, fragrant tulip with a colourful but not garish flower. Flames of purplish red flick up the outside of the orange petals, which form a bowl-shaped flower, like a cauldron sitting on an open fire. The red in the flower comes from 'Couleur Cardinal', of which this is a sport. It was registered in 1949, has the AGM, and is still very popular. There are several sports of 'Prinses Irene' including 'Hermitage', which has red flowers flamed with orange, and 'Prinses Margriet', with a yellow flower and purple flame.

GROUP Triumph
HEIGHT 35 cm (14 inches)
BLOOM TIME Mid-spring
CULTIVATION Plant in a sunny position in free-draining soil or grow in a container.
LANDSCAPE AND DESIGN USES With its short, sturdy stem, this tulip is the perfect size for a container. It also makes a good bedding plant, as long as it is planted on its own or with other tulips of similar height to maintain an even display. I think it would look wonderful with 'Couleur Cardinal', the red and plum purple flowers matching the flames on 'Prinses Irene'.
ALTERNATIVES 'Hermitage' is probably the nearest in colour to 'Prinses Irene' among the Triumph tulips and another sport, 'Orange Princess', is the same colour but in a double flower.

Tulipa 'Brown Sugar'

The unusual and unique colour of the flower is not found in many other tulips and really is the colour of brown sugar. In certain light you could even imagine the petals have been crafted out of bronze. The colour is deeper towards the centre of each gently rounded petal and inside the flower are a small, dull yellow blotch and a cluster of dark purple anthers. The petals form a cup shape, with the outer three petals peeling back first as the flower opens up. This is not a bright tulip, but it has an intriguing colour that draws your eye.

GROUP Triumph

HEIGHT 45 cm (18 inches)

BLOOM TIME Mid-spring

CULTIVATION Grow in a sunny border with fertile, well-drained soil but lift the bulbs for the summer.

LANDSCAPE AND DESIGN USES The unusual colour of 'Brown Sugar' makes an intriguing display on its own, but this tulip really needs a companion for some contrast. It goes well with red tulips and flowering mid-season means there are plenty to choose from, such as 'Red Shine' in the Lily-flowered Group, 'Apeldoorn' in the Darwin Hybrid Group, or other Triumph tulips like 'Ile de France'. Needless to say, it is best in bedding or a large container.

ALTERNATIVES Another orange Triumph tulip is 'Cairo' but it is a brighter colour, with hints of red and purple on the outer petals or you could substitute 'Prinses Irene' but neither of these has that unusual brown hue in the flower.

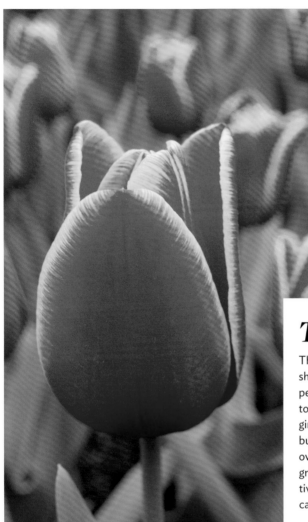

Tulipa 'Devenish'

The petals are a sophisticated blend of dusky red and pink shades with a bright, contrasting edge. The outside of each petal is red with a dusting of purple bloom, fading to orange towards the edges and highlighted with a bright yellow margin. 'Devenish' could easily be placed among the red tulips but I think the yellow margin lightens the red and gives an overall impression of a deep orange flower. The neat, grey-green leaves are pointed and held upright. This alluring cultivar was registered in 2007 and is now working its way into catalogues.

GROUP Triumph

HEIGHT 35 cm (14 inches)

BLOOM TIME Mid-spring

CULTIVATION Well-drained soil in a sunny position is perfect for this tulip but lift the bulbs for the summer.

LANDSCAPE AND DESIGN USES This new tulip will make a great partner to some of the deep purple cultivars, like 'National Velvet' or 'Havran'. Alternatively, for a brighter design, plant it with a yellow tulip to bring out the yellow along the petal edges or an orange like 'Prinses Irene' to complement the blend of colours found in the flower of 'Devenish'.

ALTERNATIVES There are similarities with 'Gavota', which has a wider yellow margin around deep reddish purple petals.

Tulipa 'Orange Princess'

'Orange Princess' is a double form of 'Prinses Irene', in the same vibrant mix of colours but with the addition of flashes of green near the tips of some of the petals. It is, of course, a sport of 'Prinses Irene' so is a similar height and flowers at the same time. Being double, the flowers are fatter, packed with oval petals, and held on a thick, sturdy stem. The cultivar was named in 1983 and it has the AGM. It has also given rise to a sport of its own, 'Red Princess', which also has the AGM. All three tulips form a royal lineage that is well worth growing.

GROUP Double Late

HEIGHT 35 cm (14 inches)

BLOOM TIME Mid to late spring

CULTIVATION Plant in sun and fertile, free-draining soil and lift for the summer or replace with new bulbs.

LANDSCAPE AND DESIGN USES In a container or bedding the wide double blooms of 'Orange Princess' make a fine, long-lasting display. Most Double Late tulips are taller but you can mix it with 'Red Princess', which is the same height, for a deep red and orange design.

ALTERNATIVES Double Late tulips come in many colours, but few are orange. The nearest to 'Orange Princess' that I have found for sale is the pale orange to yellow 'Charming Lady', which is also a similar height.

Tulipa 'Dordogne'

One of that wonderful family of pastel tulips that has arisen from the carmine red 'Renown', this tulip is a sport of the salmon pink 'Menton' but the pale orange in the petal margins of that tulip has spread to cover most of the flower in 'Dordogne'. The base of each petal is rosy pink to red, fading to subtle orange over the rest of the petal except the very tip, which is golden yellow. Inside, the flower has a yellow base and yellow anthers. This tall, elegant tulip was registered in 1991, and like 'Menton', it has the AGM.

GROUP Single Late
HEIGHT 65 cm (26 inches)
BLOOM TIME Late spring
CULTIVATION Plant it in a sunny site. Bulbs are best lifted for the summer or replaced every year to keep the flowers coming.
LANDSCAPE AND DESIGN USES The colourful but subtle shades of the flower don't look out of place in a mixed border. This tall, late-spring bedding tulip looks great with 'Avignon' and 'Menton' or 'Queen of Night'.
ALTERNATIVES 'Menton' or 'Avignon' could both be used as alternatives, the former being pinker and the latter a deeper, stronger colour with more red in the flower. Other Single Late tulips with some orange in their colour include 'Stunning Apricot' and the deep pinkish red-and-orange 'Temple's Favourite'.

Tulipa 'Little Princess'

'Little Princess' and 'Little Beauty' are a pair of charming dwarf tulips, this one a hybrid of *T. orphanidea* and *T. aucheriana* (synonym *T. humilis*). Like 'Little Beauty', it has a dark blotch in the centre of the flower with a smudged yellow margin, but in 'Little Princess' the rest of the flower is a coppery orange inside and orange with red staining on the outside. More than one stem can be produced from each bulb to produce a little cluster of flowers. This delightful, warm-coloured tulip was named in 1991 and has the AGM.

GROUP Miscellaneous
HEIGHT 10 cm (4 inches)
BLOOM TIME Mid-spring
CULTIVATION Plant in a sunny spot in free-draining soil, where it can be left to clump up naturally.
LANDSCAPE AND DESIGN USES A low-growing tulip, it is ideal for the front of a border in a gravel garden or on a rock garden or raised bed. It is the perfect companion to purple-flowered 'Little Beauty' or *T. humilis*, which is similar in size and form.
ALTERNATIVES Various forms of *T. humilis* could be alternatives to 'Little Princess' especially those sold under the name *T. kurdica*, which has brick red flowers. *Tulipa orphanidea* has reddish flowers with the same dark blotch and smudged yellow margin but is a taller plant.

Tulipa orphanidea Whittallii Group

SYNONYM *Tulipa whittallii*

I think this is one of the best, if not the best, tulip species that can be grown in the open garden. Gorgeous blooms of dusky orange are held on slender stems above the narrow leaves. The neat flower is a rounded bowl, shaped from the overlapping pointed petals. The outer three petals are coloured pale beige on their outer surface, but inside the flower is bright but not glossy orange and at the centre is a small, fuzzy, dark olive blotch with a paler margin. Originally called *T. whittallii*, this tulip was found on the hills around Izmir in western Turkey by Edward Whittall in the late nineteenth century. It was not named until 1929 but is now included within the variable *T. orphanidea*. It has the AGM.

GROUP Miscellaneous
HEIGHT 30 cm (12 inches)
BLOOM TIME Mid to late spring
CULTIVATION Coming from the Mediterranean coast of Turkey, this tulip likes a hot, dry summer but it is surprisingly adaptable to cooler, wetter regions.
LANDSCAPE AND DESIGN USES As well as the obvious places, like a rock garden or gravel garden, it can be grown successfully, without lifting, in a sunny border, as long as the soil is not too wet in summer. It is not tall so needs an open, sunny position away from taller plants but the wonderful blooms are worth every effort to accommodate.
ALTERNATIVES *Tulipa orphanidea* is a variable species but most forms are a shade of red or dark orange. No others are the dusky orange brown of this tulip but those sometimes sold under the name *T. hageri*, are equally adaptable to the garden.

GROWING
AND
PROPAGATING

Loose tulip bulbs for sale. Once in the ground they will grow roots and then a shoot from the pointed tip.

W

When you buy a packet of tulip bulbs from a garden shop or online, the bulbs are all ready to grow. The bud has already formed in the middle of the bulb and the bulb scales are full of food to feed the emerging plant. The bulbs can stay like this for several months over the summer and, if you keep them cool and dry, you can wait until the middle of winter before planting and they will still bloom in the spring. It is generally best to plant the bulbs in late autumn. This varies according to climate but will be November in the United Kingdom. In regions where winters are especially cold and the ground freezes solid for lengthy periods, the bulbs should be planted once nighttime temperatures start falling to near freezing point. It is the cold that starts root growth from the bulb and if they are planted early they can sit in damp soil for too long before growing. This can lead to the bulbs rotting.

Once the bulbs are planted and are exposed to cold and moisture, they will start to grow and can be left on their own as long as they don't dry out. Planted in the garden, new tulip bulbs will do what they're meant to do with little intervention from you.

You only need to plant a tulip bulb 5 cm (2 inches) deep and it will grow and flower, but if you want your bulbs to last from one year to the next you need to pay more attention to planting depth, soil condition, nutritional needs, water, and pests and diseases. Also, if you live in an area where hard, penetrating frosts are common, you will need to plant the bulbs deep to protect them from freezing solid. Tulips are very hardy, but you don't want to let the bulbs be completely frozen when they are in wet soil.

Hardiness

Most wild tulips grow in areas where winters are very cold. In fact, they need a cold winter and you are more likely to have problems getting bulbs to flower for more than a year in a climate where the temperature doesn't drop below freezing. This natural ability to survive a hard winter has been carried through to the garden cultivars, and tulips can be grown in most temperate climates where frosts are common. In the United States, tulips can be grown in USDA hardiness zones 3 to 8 and there should be no problem anywhere in the United Kingdom or most of Europe.

A covering of snow is an advantage in very cold climates, as its acts like a blanket, protecting the ground from extremely low temperatures, keeping it at around freezing point. Repeated freezing and thawing are more problematic because when the snow thaws it exposes the ground to air temperatures that can subsequently drop well below freezing. The water in the soil can freeze to a depth that reaches the bulbs, hence the need to plant tulips deep in these conditions.

Planting Depth and Spacing

The usual advice on planting bulbs is to bury them at a depth three times the height of the bulb. This is perfectly good for tulips, but deeper planting has its advantages, especially in regions with very cold winters. To protect them from deep frosts, the bulbs should be planted 15–20 cm (6–8 inches) deep or more. If winters are relatively mild, with just a few degrees of frost at night, then you can plant the bulbs 10–15 cm (4–6 inches) deep.

Mid-spring bulb companions of *Tulipa acuminata* and *T. linifolia* include *Narcissus* 'Polar Ice' and *Muscari neglectum*.

In a bedding scheme that is going to be dug up in early summer, the bulbs can be planted nearer the surface so they are easier to lift after flowering. However, if you leave the bulbs in the ground, in a mixed border for example, they are more likely to divide if planted too shallow. Near the ground surface the bulbs are more exposed to fluctuations in temperature, which can lead to their splitting into two or more bulbs, only one of which is usually flowering size. The smaller bulbs will not bloom or if they do, the flower will be small and the stem shorter and weaker. Planting bulbs deep protects them from more extreme fluctuations in temperature and they are less likely to split in this way.

Space bulbs 10–12 cm (4–5 inches) apart for a compact group, as you would grow in a spring bedding scheme. In a mixed border, the planting distance can vary. Tight clusters of bulbs can give way to wider spacing as the tulips spread through the border. These clusters can be planted to fill gaps in the border, joined by the scattering of bulbs between them. This variable spacing gives a sense of a naturally occurring population.

Soil and Light

Choosing the best position in the garden to plant tulips is not just about the amount of sunlight they will receive or the plants they will be growing with, it is also about the soil in which they will be growing. This is the most important aspect to consider. As a rule, tulips do best in fertile, well-drained soil that is neutral to alkaline. They need plenty of water when they are in growth, from autumn to late spring. It is when they have died down for the summer and are dormant that good drainage is important. If the soil is too wet and holds onto moisture, there is a possibility that the bulbs can rot.

Well drained doesn't mean the soil is completely dry, but rather that it allows excess water to drain away. It is perfectly possible to grow tulips in a climate with summer rain, as long as the soil drains freely. You don't have to emulate the dry, rocky slopes where tulip species grow naturally to be able to grow most garden tulips, although some of the species do need complete protection from summer rain in cultivation. For most tulip cultivars, any good garden soil is fine.

Planting bulbs close together will result in a packed display, with the blooms jostling for position, like this vivid carpet of the Darwin Hybrid tulip 'Niigata'.

Tulipa 'Ruby Red' growing in deep, fertile, free-draining soil in a sunny mixed border

If the soil in your garden is heavy and poorly drained, you can amend it to improve the drainage. Organic matter, such as composted green waste or well-rotted manure, can be added to clay soil to open up the texture. Mixing in grit or sand will also help improve the movement of water through the soil.

When amending soil for planting tulips, you will have to dig deep enough to ensure that drainage below the bulbs is improved. That means digging at least 30 cm (12 inches) down and ideally more. Raising the planting bed above ground level by constructing a rock garden or raised bed will also ensure water drains freely.

Another way to improve drainage around the bulb is to plant it on a layer of sharp sand. Dig a hole for the bulb and add some sand at the bottom. Place the bulb on the sand and then fill the hole with soil again, firming lightly. It is round the basal plate, from which the roots grow, that rot often starts to take hold. Placing the bulb on sand helps to keep excess moisture away from this part of the bulb.

If you have good garden soil, the other main consideration when choosing where to plant tulips is the amount of sunlight they receive. A sunny border is best. In the Northern Hemisphere, this means a south- or southwest-facing border or an open position not shaded by walls, hedges, or taller plants. Growing near or under deciduous trees is acceptable because the tulips are in growth when the trees are bare. Only once the tulips are dying down will the leaves on the trees shut out direct sunlight, and once the trees are in growth they will take excess moisture out of the ground, keeping the soil reasonably dry.

Feeding tulips at the beginning of their growing season will encourage the formation of strong, healthy bulbs for flowering the next year. With a new tulip bulb being formed every year, it is important to ensure there are enough nutrients in the soil for that new bulb to form. A lack of nutrients will result in a smaller, weaker bulb. If you have added organic matter to the soil, especially well-rotted manure, then this will provide the nutrients needed by the bulbs. Alternatively, you can sprinkle feed, such as bone meal or chicken manure pellets, into the soil when planting, or water in feed around the tulips as they appear above ground. A low-nitrogen liquid feed, like that appropriate for tomato food, will encourage good bud and bulb formation. Avoid high-nitrogen feed, which can encourage leafy growth at the expense of flowers. If you are lucky enough to have deep, fertile soil, then added feed won't do any harm but is not so important unless the bulbs are showing signs of reduced vigour.

Lift or Leave?

The decision whether to lift the bulbs for the summer or leave them in the ground depends on the type of planting scheme, the climate and planting location, and the type of tulip. Lifting the bulbs ensures they have a completely dry summer rest. It also allows you to sort them according to size and check for any disease.

Larger bulbs can be replanted in autumn and are likely to flower. The smaller bulbs and offsets can then be planted out of the way, lined out in a corner of the garden where

These bulbs of 'Moonshine' revel in the free-draining soil, warmth, and sunshine at the foot of a brick garden wall.

Tulipa saxatilis 'Lilac Wonder' underplanted with a mixture of Greek windflowers (*Anemone blanda*)

they can be allowed to grow and build up strength. The following summer they can be lifted and, if large enough, added to the main display or border.

Dig the bulbs up carefully as they are dying down. The leaves will brown from their tip and when this extends down most of the leaf, the bulbs can be lifted. Leaving them until the leaves have completely died and become detached makes the bulbs much harder to find, especially if they are mixed in with other plants that you do not want to disturb.

Once lifted, clean off the soil and lay the bulbs with their leaves still attached in a cool, dry place. Do not remove the leaves until they have completely dried up, then twist them away from the bulb; there should be little resistance. There is no need to remove the brown tunic around the bulb but it will do no harm; some grower's like to remove the tunic in case it is harbouring fungal spores.

Sort the bulbs and store them in net or paper bag, in a cool, dry location out of sunlight. The ideal temperature to store bulbs is 18–20°C (65–68°F). The nets or bags of bulbs can be hung from the roof inside a shed or garage, to ensure they are dry but have good ventilation to discourage fungal diseases. It is important to protect them from pests, such as mice, that will eat the bulbs if they can get to them.

You will have to lift bulbs if you have garden soil that is not well-drained and remains wet all summer or if you only want the biggest, most reliable flowering bulbs growing in your borders. If you are content with variability in the tulip flowers and the possibility that they might not flower at all, and your soil is free draining or you live in an area with naturally dry summers, then leaving them in the ground year-round is not a problem. The variation makes for a more naturalistic effect and you can always add a few new bulbs of the same cultivar each year to boost the display.

Tulips for Permanent Plantings

Darwin Hybrid Group
Fosteriana Group
Greigii Group
Kaufmanniana Group
Some Lily-flowered tulips
Some species tulips

Tulips Best Lifted and Stored Dry

Triumph Group
Fringed Group
Parrot Group
Single Early Group
Single Late Group
Double tulips

Pests and Diseases

The two main diseases to look out for on tulips are tulip fire, which is a fungal disease, and viruses, which are spread by aphids or nematodes. Slugs can also be a problem, especially the small black slugs that live in the soil. They can eat through the leaves and bud before they have even emerged from the ground

Tulip fire is spread by the fungus *Botrytis tulipae* and can quickly kill a tulip collection in a short space of time. It usually occurs if the soil is too wet or the atmosphere too still and damp. Spots appear on the leaves and flower above ground and on the bulb underground. Look out for it if you lift the bulbs in summer, but it is more obvious on the leaves and stem, which will become twisted and distorted. As they die, a grey mould

Early signs of tulip fire on *Tulipa* 'Little Princess'

Tulipa 'China Pink' showing the effect of tulip breaking virus

can appear on the dead tissue. The spots can also appear on the flowers, which can rot quickly in wet weather.

Small black structures called sclerotia, appear on the dead tissue and can infect the soil so new, healthy bulbs will also be affected as they emerge. Air-borne spores spread the disease to exposed part of the plant.

To treat this disease you will have to remove any infected bulbs and all the above-ground parts of the plant. Do not replant tulips in the same space for at least three years. It is very important to get rid of any infected plants quickly to avoid the disease spreading. Ensuring the soil is well drained and the tulips are planted in a location that has good air movement helps to prevent the disease occurring. Removing the flower petals as they fade is also important.

Several viruses can affect tulips. The symptoms show as streaking or mottling on the leaves and in the case of tulip breaking virus, the flower colour becomes broken up and patterned. Aphids, or greenfly, that suck the sap from the plant, can spread the viruses to other plants, not just tulips. A tulip may live for several years with a virus but apart from the risk of the virus spreading to other plants, it will gradually weaken the tulip it has infected. The only way to stop the spread is to remove the infected plant and destroy it. Killing the aphids will help but they reproduce very quickly and it only takes one to infect another plant. Some viruses are spread by nematodes in the soil and again, only destroying the plant will remove the virus.

Luckily, tulips are largely disease free if you give them the right conditions. An open sunny position in fertile, free-draining soil will lessen the chances of any fungal diseases occurring and prompt removal of any plants that show signs of virus will reduce the chance of other plants being infected. It is likely that some tulips left in the ground to flower every spring will eventually succumb to virus so keep a good look out for any signs and remove the affected plants. Of course, discarding old tulips and buying new bulbs every year can overcome many of these problems but it is still worth checking the bulbs for signs of disease before you plant them. Above all, don't let this put you off growing tulips. Many people grow thousands of tulips every year without any issues, just keep an eye out for any abnormalities while you enjoy their beautiful flowers.

Propagation

Tulips can be propagated vegetatively, by the production of small bulbs called offsets, or from seed. Tulip species will usually produce seed but the cultivars often do not or the seeds are the result of hybridizing between different tulips in your garden so the new plants will not be the same as the one from which you collected the seed. If you plant bulbs in a border, they will naturally increase anyway, in the right conditions.

For most gardeners, there is little need to propagate tulips, as new bulbs are readily available and buying them new also provides the opportunity to try new cultivars and planting ideas. If you want to bulk up the numbers of an existing cultivar that you are growing, then you can encourage the production of offsets but it can be a slow process to get them to flowering size.

A tulip plant showing the old bulb with its brown tunic and new bulbs forming as stolons. The old bulb will disappear to be replaced by the new.

The thin, papery seeds of a tulip are released from the brittle seedpods.

When you dig up bulbs from the bedding scheme or empty them out of a container at the end of spring, the bulbs may well have divided into a cluster of smaller bulbs or off-sets. Only the largest is likely to flower and it is possible that none will be flowering size. This is normally the opposite of what you want to happen and replanting them at the right depth will reduce their tendency to split in this way.

Shallow planting will expose the bulb to fluctuations in temperature and this encourages them to divide. If you want to increase your bulbs then this behaviour can be used to your advantage. Plant them shallow and then dig them up in spring and you should have more than you put in. Store them somewhere with a stable temperature, if possible, over the summer and replant them deeper in the autumn to let them build up strength.

It can take a few years of lifting, feeding, and replanting to get them to flowering size and unless you can provide that stable, unfluctuating temperature during the summer the bulbs can still split, prolonging the time it takes them to flower. Let's face it, this is probably best left to the professionals. The Dutch have perfected the art of lifting and storing bulbs. They have the expertise and facilities to do this on a huge scale and the resulting bulbs are remarkably cheap considering the effort that goes into producing them so take advantage and buy them new.

Tulip species will also increase by division of the bulb and some produce stolons and spread remarkably quickly. By lifting healthy clumps every few years you can spread them around and gradually increase the area they cover but in most cases it is best to let

Tulip seedlings in a seed pot

Tulipa sprengeri can self-sow
its seed and gradually colonize
part of the garden.

the tulips do their own thing. The best way to increase the species is from seed, although there is still the chance of hybridization if you have more than one species growing together.

In the centre of a tulip flower is the ovary and as the petals fade, the ovary develops into the seedpod. It will go brown and then split open to reveal the flat, papery seeds. Collect them and keep them dry until you are ready to sow. Choose a pot that is not too shallow, at least 10 cm (4 inches) deep. Fill to near the top with a fine soil mix, firm lightly, and scatter the seeds over the surface. Don't sow too many in one pot and try not to let the seeds overlap. Then sieve some more soil over the seeds to cover them. A thin mulch of fine grit will protect the soil surface when watering.

The first time you water the pot, leave it in a tray of water to soak up the moisture. Once you can see that the top of the soil is moist, you know that the pot has enough water. Keep the pot cool and shaded outside, and don't let it dry out.

Germination of the seed normally occurs during the winter or early spring, once the seeds have been exposed to a cold period. What you must not do is prick-out the seedlings as soon as they appear. They will look like a thin grassy leaf. Because the tiny new bulb needs time to form, leave the seedlings in their pot for at least a year. They will die down in late spring but still keep the soil just moist; the new bulb cannot cope with a very dry summer yet.

The leaves will reappear the next winter and the young plants will benefit from a weak liquid feed to help them build up strength. If you think they look strong enough, then once they have died down a second time, you can tip them out and plant them into a larger container. Do this every summer until they are large enough to plant in the garden. It can take four years or more to reach flowering size but you will have a lot more bulbs that you started with.

A few species will increase by seed without your intervention and the best at this is *Tulipa sprengeri*. This species produces abundant seed, which if left to fall naturally, will germinate around the parent plant. You will see thin grasslike leaves appearing in spring and a few years later they will be flowering.

Planting in Containers

Growing tulips in containers is one of the easiest ways to enjoy these bulbs. You don't have to find the right spot in your garden, worry about the surrounding plants, or amend the soil to improve drainage. A range of different containers can be used, from large, rustic terracotta pots to glazed urns or a large trough, as long as they are deep enough and in scale with the tulips you plant in them. For tulip cultivars, the container needs to be at least 30 cm (12 inches) deep to allow the bulbs to be planted at a reasonable depth and leave room for the roots. The container must have holes in the bottom to allow excess water to drain away.

The soil used to fill the container should be free draining of course, but you can buy soil for this purpose. Choose a loam-based soil with grit or sand mixed in or buy specially

Planting tulip bulbs in a container. After planting, the container is topped up with soil and watered.

produced bulb compost, sometimes called bulb fibre. Fill the container to half or two thirds of its depth with the soil and place the bulbs on the surface. To improve drainage around the bulb, you could place a layer of sharp sand on the soil. This will keep the basal plate, from which the roots grow, dry and help prevent rot from taking hold.

Bulbs in a container can be planted close together—even closer than when planted in the ground—as long as they don't touch each other. They will erupt out of the pot to form a stunning cluster of colour, but they will need removing once finished and planted elsewhere to give them room to grow.

Cover the bulbs with more soil to within about 1 cm (0.5 inch) of the rim. The soil can be covered with mulch, such as grit, to keep wet soil away from the leaves of the tulips, and it looks more attractive.

Water the soil well, until water can be seen draining out of the bottom. This ensures the soil is wet throughout the container. Afterwards, just keep the soil moist until the tulips appear, after which you can water more frequently. It is very important never to let the soil dry out completely when the tulips are in growth.

The bulbs should only be grown for one year in this soil, so wide spacing is not necessary. In fact, you can layer two varieties of bulb in one container, with a second tulip or a different type of bulb, planted in a layer above the first, as long as you don't place one bulb directly above another. Once the tulips start to die down, reduce the amount of water they are given and when they have retreated completely underground, stop watering. Tip out the soil and bulbs, and replant them in the garden. New soil should be used in

Tulips for a Container

Tulipa 'Ancilla'
Tulipa 'Apricot Beauty'
Tulipa 'Calgary'
Tulipa 'Candy Prince'
Tulipa 'Couleur Cardinal'
Tulipa 'Flair'
Tulipa 'Paul Rubens'
Tulipa 'Pieter de Leur'
Tulipa 'Prinses Irene'
Tulipa 'Rococo'
Tulipa 'Russian Princess'
Tulipa 'Showwinner'
Tulipa 'Van der Neer'

Tulips for a Large Container

Tulipa 'Ballerina'
Tulipa 'Havran'
Tulipa 'Ivory Floradale'
Tulipa 'Queen of Night'
Tulipa 'Red Princess'
Tulipa 'Red Spring Green'
Tulipa 'Renown'
Tulipa 'White Triumphator'
Tulipa 'World's Favourite'

Tulipa 'Flaming Flag' grown in a terracotta pot

A cold frame can be used to protect pots from rain and freezing temperatures.

Tulipa 'Ballade' planted in a border, having been transferred from a container after their first year

The early flowers of *Tulipa biflora* can be damaged by early spring weather but given the protection of a cold frame or cool glasshouse they form perfect, unblemished stars.

a container every year as it will become exhausted of nutrients after one season and can harbour disease.

It is important to when planting tulips in containers to protect the bulbs from completely freezing in wet soil. The container will need to be given protection from hard frosts to prevent it freezing right through. One way to protect containers of planted bulbs is to keep them in a cold frame, with the lid, or frame light, closed during cold weather. This provides a couple of degrees of protection. Burying pots of planted bulbs up to their rim in sand, inside the frame, gives further protection, as the sides of the pot are not exposed.

A cool glasshouse can give greater shelter from extreme cold and can be heated to keep the temperature inside close to or just above freezing point. This type of glasshouse is usually used to grow alpine plants. Alpines are also frost hardy but pots of moist soil can freeze solid without some shelter.

If you do not have a glasshouse or cold frame, you can store the pots in a shed or garage but as soon as the leaves appear above the soil level the plants will need to be brought into the light, otherwise they will become etiolated—drawn up in search of the sun. Placing these containers next to a sunny house wall or in an open porch will provide a little extra warmth, while allowing light to the tulips as they grow.

Growing Species Tulips

Growing tulip species is a little different from growing the garden cultivars. Most need free-draining soil, good air movement, and a sunny position, even more so than the cultivars. There are a few exceptions, such as *Tulipa sprengeri*, that can be grown in a more shaded position and in soil that does retain moisture in the summer, but the vast majority need a dry summer rest and many of them should not have any water at all at this time.

Most tulip species are not suited to bedding, due to their smaller size and relatively short flowering period, but there are some wonderful plants among them, including several good garden plants. In the right position they will build up a small colony over time.

Planting the small bulbs of *Tulips clusiana* in late autumn on a layer of sand in a pot of gritty soil

Cover the planted bulbs with more soil.

The pot filled with soil

Cover the surface of the soil with a mulch of grit to protect the soil surface and keep the leaves of the tulip away from the wet soil.

Four or five months after planting, the
bulbs of *Tulipa clusiana* will be flowering.

Tulipa clusiana on a small
rock garden built on a low,
sunny slope

Tulipa kaufmanniana growing on the Rock Garden at the Royal Botanic Gardens, Kew

The bulbs of these species are better not lifted for this reason, as disturbing them every year will interrupt their natural inclination to increase.

Plant tulip species at least 10 cm (4 inches) deep, more for larger bulbs like *Tulipa fosteriana*, with a layer of sharp sand at the bottom of the planting hole to aid drainage around the base of the bulb. The better the drainage, the more tulips you should be able to grow successfully outside. That is important, as their ability to live for many years without being disturbed is part of their appeal.

Although tulip species are very hardy, some of them, like *Tulipa biflora*, flower early in the season and their flowers can be damaged by cold wind and rain. Once you have found the right position outdoors, they can be left to do their thing except for some feed scattered over the soil or watered in, to promote vigorous, healthy growth, especially in well-established clumps that have become congested.

Even if you can't accommodate tulip species in your garden, they are worth growing in pots and they won't take up much room. Planting in pots is also the way to grow species that need a completely dry summer, as once they have died down they can be moved to where they are sheltered from the rain—in a well-ventilated cool glasshouse or cold frame—before repotting them in late summer or autumn. The smaller tulip species can be grown in relatively small pots, making them ideal if space is limited. Keep them in the sun but make sure you water often when the tulips are growing because smaller pots will dry out quickly. The critical point is when the leaves start to brown. This is when to reduce watering so the soil is just moist. Once dormant, the pot should be left to dry out completely.

Cut Flowers

If you like tulips in your garden, then eventually you will want some in your house and tulips make wonderful cut flowers. The majority of commercially grown tulips are for the cut flower trade and these have been selected for their relatively stout, rigid stems but they will continue to grow once picked and put in water. This habit of continuing to elongate once the stems are cut can be used to create bizarre flower arrangements using tulips from your garden. Tall varieties with long, thin stems will bend over as they stretch themselves in a vase. The flower will then turn upright as it leans towards the light, causing a twisting stem that never quite stays still. A flower arrangement with tulips like this may look unruly but it makes a change from rigidly formal designs.

You can plant tulips in the garden just to provide cut flowers. Select a range of different cultivars from different groups, with varied colours and flowering times, to ensure plenty of material is available for displaying inside the house. The bulbs can be planted in lines in a discreet part of your garden, where cutting the flowers won't harm the main display or you can just make sure you plant enough bulbs in the garden that removing a few won't make a big difference. Bringing tulips inside also allows you to appreciate their scent. Their perfume isn't strong and overpowering like hyacinths or even some daffodils but having them in a vase means you are more likely to notice any fragrance than you would from plants in the garden.

If you want to exhibit tulips at a flower show, then bendy stems should be avoided. You can do this by cutting the tulips and wrapping a bunch of stems together in a roll of newspaper, held together with rubber bands or string. This will keep them straight for long enough to transport to the show and arrange in the vase for the judges. Cut the stems as near to the show time as possible so they have plenty of water and don't start to droop. Lay them down flat as they are being transported or, if it is a long journey, stand them in a narrow vase with a little water at the bottom. You should also be looking at perfect, unblemished blooms, of a good size and at the right stage of development; not so early that the petals haven't fully expanded and not so late they are beginning to fade. Cut more than you need so you have some choice when arranging them on the show bench. Remember to read the show schedule carefully. Exhibiting the wrong number of stems or choosing tulips from the wrong division will lead to instant disqualification but getting it right and winning a medal or even just the excitement of competing, is a great feeling.

Tulips for Cut Flowers

Tulipa 'China Pink'
Tulipa 'Ivory Floradale'
Tulipa 'Parrot Lady'
Tulipa 'Red Georgette'

de Jager Flower Bulbs
188 Asbury Street
South Hamilton, Massachsetss 01982
www.dejagerflowerbulbs.com

Eden Brothers
34 Old Brevard Road
Asheville, North Carolina 28806
www.edenbrothers.com

John Scheepers
23 Tulip Drive
Bantam, Connecticut 06750
www.johnscheepers.com

Old House Gardens
536 Third St.
Ann Arbor, Michigan 48103
www.oldhousegardens.com
Antique "broken" tulips

Tulips.com
P.O.Box 1248
Mount Vernon, Washington 98273
www.tulips.com

TulipWorld
8480 North 87th Street
Milwaukee, Wisconsin 53223
www.tulipworld.com

Van Bourgondien
PO Box 309
Cleves, Ohio 45002
www.dutchbulbs.com

White Flower Farm
167 Litchfield Road
Morris, Connecticut 06763
www.whiteflowerfarm.com

WHERE TO SEE

In town centres, suburban streets, parks and gardens you are bound to see tulips flowering in spring, usually planted in bedding schemes or raised beds and roundabouts. After daffodils, they must be the most often-planted spring bulbs. Some gardens or even whole towns make the most of the tulip flowering season by staging tulip festivals, with magnificent displays of massed tulips. Botanic gardens are the place to search out some of the tulip species, planted on a rock garden or grown in pots in an alpine house. Then there are gardens that grow tulips in mixed borders in more subtle designs where the tulips' blooms combine effortlessly with other spring flowers.

CANADA

Canadian Tulip Festival
Ottawa, Ontario
www.tulipfestival.ca

GERMANY

Mainau
78465 Insel Mainau
www.mainau.de/home.html

ITALY

Castello di Pralormo
Via Umberto I, 26
10040 Pralormo (TO)
www.castellodipralormo.com

The Gardens of Trauttmansdorff Castle
Via S. Valentino 51a
Merano
http://www.trauttmansdorff.it

Parco Giardino Sigurtà
Via Cavour 1
37067 Valeggio sul Mincio (Verona)
www.sigurta.it

NETHERLANDS

Hortus Bulborum Foundation
Zuidkerkenlaan 23A
1906 AC Limmen
www.hortus-bulborum.nl

Keukenhof
Stationsweg 166A
2161 AM Lisse
www.keukenhof.nl/en

UNITED KINGDOM

Abbey House Gardens
Malmesbury
Wiltshire
England SN16 9AS
www.abbeyhousegardens.co.uk

Cambo House and Gardens
Kingsbarns
St. Andrews
Fife
Scotland KY16 8QD
www.camboestate.com/gardens

Cambridge University Botanic Garden
1 Brookside
Cambridge
England CB2 1JE
www.botanic.cam.ac.uk

Chenies Manor House
Rickmansworth
Buckinghamshire
England WD3 6ER
www.cheniesmanorhouse.co.uk

Eden Project
Bodelva
Cornwall
England PL24 2SG
www.edenproject.com

Great Dixter House and Garden
Northiam
Rye
East Sussex
England TN31 6PH
www.greatdixter.co.uk

Pashley Manor Gardens
Ticehurst
Near Wadhurst
East Sussex
England TN5 7HE
www.pashleymanorgardens.com

RHS Garden Wisley
Woking
Surrey
England GU23 6QB
www.rhs.org.uk/gardens/wisley

Royal Botanic Gardens Kew
Richmond
Surrey
England TW9 3AB
http://www.kew.org

Royal Botanic Garden Edinburgh
Inverleith Row
Arboretum Place
Edinburgh
Scotland EH3 5LR
www.rbge.org.uk

Sizergh Castle
near Kendal
Cumbria
England LA8 8AE
www.nationaltrust.org.uk/sizergh

Springfields Festival Gardens
Spalding
Lincolnshire
England
www.springfieldsgardens.co.uk

UNITED STATES

Atlanta Botanical Garden
1345 Piedmont Ave NE
Atlanta, Georgia 30309
www.atlantabotanicalgarden.org

Denver Botanic Gardens
1007 York Street
Denver, Colorado 80206
www.botanicgardens.org

New York Botanical Garden
2900 Southern Boulevard
Bronx, New York 10458
www.nybg.org

Skagit Valley Tulip Festival
Mt. Vernon, Washington
www.tulipfestival.org

Tulip Time Festival
Holland, Michigan
www.tuliptime.com

Veldheer Tulip Gardens
12755 Quincy St.
Holland, Michigan 49424
www.veldheer.com

FOR MORE INFORMATION

BOOKS

Everett, Diana. 2013. *The Genus* Tulipa*: Tulips of the World*. Richmond, Surrey: Kew Publishing.

Heath, Brent and Becky. 2001. *Tulips for North American Gardens*. Houston, Texas: Bright Sky Press.

King, Michael. 2005. *Gardening with Tulips*. London: Frances Lincoln.

Lloyd, Christopher. 2004. *Christopher Lloyd's Gardening Year*. London: Frances Lincoln.

Pavord, Anna. 2000. *The Tulip*. London: Bloomsbury Publishing.

Skelmersdale, Christine. 2012. *A Gardener's Guide to Bulbs*. Marlborough, England: Crowood Press.

Wilford, Richard. 2006. *Tulips: Species and Hybrids for the Gardener*. Portland, Oregon: Timber Press.

WEBSITES

The Royal General Bulb Growers' Association (KAVB): www.kavb.nl

The Tulip Gallery: www.thetulipgallery.com

ORGANIZATIONS

Alpine Garden Society: www.alpinegardensociety.net

International Bulb Society: www.bulbsociety.org

Pacific Bulb Society: www.pacificbulbsociety.org

Royal Horticultural Society: www.rhs.org.uk

Wakefield & North of England Tulip Society: www.tulipsociety.co.uk

PHOTO CREDITS

Photographs are by the author unless indicated otherwise.

COVER: (front and back bottom row) Brent and Becky Heath; (spine) John Scheepers.

BOTANIKFOTO/STEFFEN HAUSER, page 108.
BRENT AND BECKY HEATH OF BRENT AND BECKY'S BULBS, pages 39, 40–41, 50 lower right, 53 left, 53, 57 upper left, 57 lower right, 63 right, 66–67, 72, 74, 75, 81, 88, 89, 92, 98 left, 109, 124, 130, 131, 134, 137, 146, 148, 159, 160, 170, 182–183, 185, 189 left.
GAP/JONATHAN BUCKLEY, page 43.
IBULB.ORG, page 136.
IBULB.ORG/ANDREW LAWSON, page 120.
IBULB.ORG/FOTOSTUDIO ARTIFEX, page 114 left.
IBULB.ORG/F-STUDIO, pages 62 right, 73, 121 right.
IBULB.ORG/LEONTINE TRIJBER, page 180.
IBULB.ORG/MAAYKE DE RIDDER, page 83.
IBULB.ORG/STEVEN BEMELMAN, page 84 left.
IBULB.ORG/WOUTER KOPPEN, pages 59 bottom, 62 left, 65 left, 80 left, 127, 142, 144, 166.
JOHN SCHEEPERS, pages 52 left, 55, 58, 61, 79, 97, 99, 101, 106, 111, 112, 119, 125, 129, 135 right, 138, 141, 149, 151, 157, 161, 168, 171, 177, 178, 179.
KIT STRANGE, page 47 top.

INDEX

ABOUT THE AUTHOR

RICHARD WILFORD has worked at the Royal Botanic Gardens, Kew, for 26 years. He has a particular interest in bulbs and is a member of the Royal Horticultural Society's Bulb Committee (formally the Daffodil and Tulip Committee). He has written numerous articles for *Kew Magazine, Gardens Illustrated,* and *Curtis's Botanical Magazine.* He is on the Publications Committee for Kew Publishing and the editorial committees of *Kew Magazine* and *Curtis's Botanical Magazine.* He is the author of *Tulips: Species and Hybrids for the Gardener,* published by Timber Press in 2006, *Alpines: From Mountain to Garden,* published by Kew in 2010, and *Growing Garden Bulbs,* also published by Kew, in 2013. All Richard's books are illustrated extensively with his photographs.

JOANNE EVERSON

The Haseltine Building   6a Lonsdale Road
133 S.W. Second Avenue, Suite 450   London NW6 6RD
Portland, Oregon 97204-3527

For details on other Timber Press books and to sign up for our newsletters, please visit our websites, timberpress.com and timberpress.co.uk.

Library of Congress Cataloging-in-Publication Data
Wilford, Richard, 1964-
  The plant lover's guide to tulips/Richard Wilford.—First edition.
    pages cm
  Includes index.
  ISBN 978-1-60469-534-2
  1. Tulips. I. Title.
  SB413.T9W54 2015
  635.9'3432—dc23
                                    2014024944

A catalogue record for this book is also available from the British Library.

Book and cover design by Laken Wright
Layout and composition by Ben Patterson
Printed in China

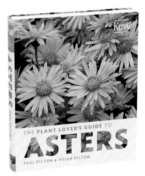